Tarot for Beginners

What You Need to Know about Reading Tarot Cards, Spreads, Astrology, Kabbalah, Divination, Psychic Development, and Numerology

© Copyright 2023 - All rights reserved.

The contents of this book may not be reproduced, duplicated, or transmitted without direct written permission from the author.

Under no circumstances will any legal responsibility or blame be held against the publisher for any reparation, damages, or monetary loss due to the information herein, either directly or indirectly.

Legal Notice:

This book is copyright protected. This is only for personal use. You cannot amend, distribute, sell, use, quote or paraphrase any part or the content within this book without the consent of the author.

Disclaimer Notice:

Please note the information contained within this document is for educational and entertainment purposes only. Every attempt has been made to provide accurate, up-to-date, reliable, and complete information. No warranties of any kind are expressed or implied. Readers acknowledge that the author is not engaging in the rendering of legal, financial, medical, or professional advice. The content of this book has been derived from various sources. Please consult a licensed professional before attempting any techniques outlined in this book.

By reading this document, the reader agrees that under no circumstances is the author responsible for any losses, direct or indirect, which are incurred as a result of the use of the information contained within this document, including, but not limited to errors, omissions, or inaccuracies.

Your Free Gift
(only available for a limited time)

Thanks for getting this book! If you want to learn more about various spirituality topics, then join Mari Silva's community and get a free guided meditation MP3 for awakening your third eye. This guided meditation mp3 is designed to open and strengthen ones third eye so you can experience a higher state of consciousness. Simply visit the link below the image to get started.

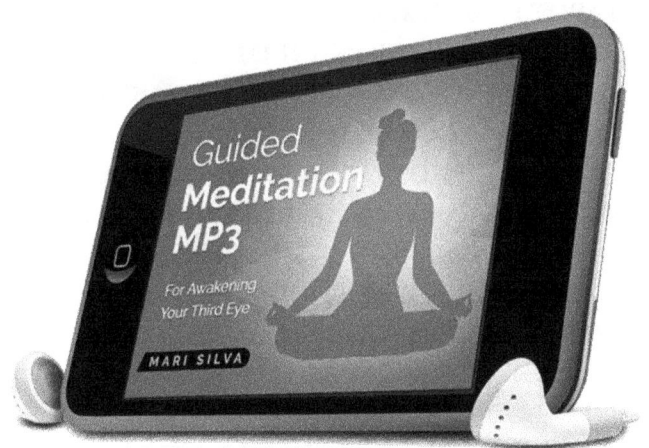

https://spiritualityspot.com/meditation

Table of Contents

INTRODUCTION 1
CHAPTER 1: TAROT BASICS 3
CHAPTER 2: DEVELOPING YOUR PSYCHIC POWERS FIRST 10
CHAPTER 3: KABBALAH AND TAROT: A MYSTICAL CONNECTION 18
CHAPTER 4: THE ASTROLOGY BEHIND TAROT 25
CHAPTER 5: THE CARDS AND NUMEROLOGY......................34
CHAPTER 6: MEET THE CARDS I: MAJOR ARCANA 41
CHAPTER 7: MEET THE CARDS II: FOUR SUITES................82
CHAPTER 8: MEET THE CARDS III: COURT CARDS.............92
CHAPTER 9: SPREADS AND LAYOUTS 96
CONCLUSION - READING THE CARDS 102
HERE'S ANOTHER BOOK BY MARI SILVA THAT YOU MIGHT LIKE...105
YOUR FREE GIFT (ONLY AVAILABLE FOR A LIMITED TIME) 106
REFERENCES..107

Introduction

The Tarot is a map of human consciousness encompassing your life's journey. Tarot card reading is the art and practice of divining wisdom and knowledge from a tarot card deck. The cards provide in-depth insights into your problems and can be used to seek solutions to these problems. The cards do not foretell anything but simply help you delve deep into your consciousness to find answers that are already embedded there.

This book combines the power of tarot cards with the esoteric knowledge of Kabbalah, the energy of numbers, and the secrets of astrology. Combining the limitless power of these divination tools, you can read tarot cards with great accuracy and find solutions and answers to questions for yourself and other's seeking a reading, referred to as querents.

The best thing about this book is that it speaks to novice and experienced readers alike. It is excellent for beginners as the basics are explained in simple, easy-to-understand language. It contains hands-on methods and instructions that you can practice daily to become an effective tarot card reader.

Tarot card reading by itself is a great tool, but when you combine it with the insights given by Kabbalistic, astrological, and numerological divination tools, then the outcome can be significantly better. This book teaches you the basics of the other three divination tools. It explains how they can be combined with the energy of a tarot card deck to get amazing results.

So, go on, turn the page, and discover the power of tarot card reading.

Chapter 1: Tarot Basics

At first glance, a dark Tarot deck may seem just like any other deck of playing cards. Well, nothing could be further from the truth. Tarot cards have been used for self-discovery, divination, and other magical, mystical purposes.

Tarot cards have been used for centuries.
https://pixabay.com/es/photos/artesan%c3%ada-tarot-adivinaci%c3%b3n-2728227/

History of Tarot Cards

The Tarot's magical calling has attracted a lot of magic practitioners for centuries. It is one of the most common divination tools humans have used for a long time. The history of tarot cards can be traced back to the 14th century in Europe. European artists are credited with creating the first tarot cards used for games only. These European artists created four suits similar to the ones in use today.

The Italians invented the tarot card deck in the 1430s. Artists added a fifth suit of 21 cards to the existing 4-suit playing card deck. The 21 newly-added, specially-designed cards were called Trionfi, Tarocchi, or "triumph." Another odd card called il Matto, or "the Fool," was also added to make the tarot deck a collection of 78 cards. Tarot cards were commonly used in Venice, Milan, Florence, and Urbino.

With the growing popularity of tarot card decks, rich Italian families such as the Visconti family of Milan began ordering customized decks to include paintings and portraits of their close friends and family members. The Italian artists created customized trump (or triumph) cards for these wealthy families.

This was an expensive affair and was restricted to the rich. One luxury tarot deck that survived from the mid-15th century is believed to have been customized for Filippo Maria Visconti, the last duke of Milan. However, with the advent of the printing press, tarot cards became more affordable, and even common citizens could enjoy using them in their homes.

Until the 16th century, tarot cards were used only to play games, especially popular in France and Italy. From around the 16th and 17th centuries, the Tarot also picked up pace as a divination tool. Yet, it was not until the 18th century that the meanings for each specific card were concretized, and layouts and spreads began to be formed.

In 1781, Antoine Court de Gebelin wrote a detailed analysis of the tarot card decks and the specific meanings and symbolism of each card. Further, he connected the symbolism and meaning to occult knowledge of ancient Egypt, especially with the legends of Egyptian gods such as Isis and Osiris. This work became very popular among the rich Europeans seeking esoteric knowledge.

Jean-Baptiste Alliette, a French occultist, countered Gebelin's work with his own theories and ideas a few years later. In his book, Alliette explained how to use the tarot card deck as a divination tool. Also, in 1791, he designed the first tarot card deck specifically created for divination rather than for playing purposes.

Divination and occult studies became very popular among rich Europeans during and after the Victorian Era. Events of the occult, such as seances and tarot card readings, were common at parties and social gatherings. Today, tarot card readings are among the most commonly used divination tools.

The Structure of a Tarot Card Deck

A Tarot card deck comprises 78 cards divided into two groups: the Major Arcana and Minor Arcana. The word Arcana is rooted in "arcane," which is, in turn, rooted in the Latin word "Arcanum," which translates to "secret or mysterious" or "something that is known or understood by very few people."

The Major Arcana, also called Trumps, consists of 22 cards and starts with Fool's card, or the Zero (0) card. The rest of them have the numbers 1 to 21 on them. Each of the 22 cards signifies a specific esoteric meaning. The Major Arcana depicts the soul's journey (represented by the Fool) as it passes through various stages of self-awareness and knowledge until it reaches possible enlightenment. The Major Arcana represent the archetypal elements people see and interact with in the world. Each archetype signifies a crucial stage of spiritual and/or psychological development.

The Minor Arcana, also called Pips, consists of 56 cards representing the "minor or small" mysteries of our lives and the world around us. This set of 56 cards is further categorized into four suits, namely:

- The Suit of Wands
- The Suit of Swords
- The Suit of Cups
- The Suit of Pentacles

Each of the four suits consists of 14 cards from numbers 1 (also called the Ace card) to 10 (10 cards) and four "court cards," including the Page, Knight, Queen, and King. While most decks have 78 cards, some have less or more. This book deals primarily with the 78-card deck. Later in this book, the Major and Minor Arcana cards are described in detail.

Types of Tarot Card Decks

The number of different types of decks available today is mind-boggling. There is a deck for every kind of practitioner and their likes or dislikes. Ranging from fandom characters to sports characters, there is no limit to the variety available today. Regardless of the pictures on the deck, each Major and Minor Arcana card's meanings and interpretations do not change. This chapter looks at some of the most basic types of tarot card decks that have withstood the test of time.

Rider-Waite

The Order of the Golden Dawn was one of Europe's most popular occult groups during the late 19th and early 20th centuries. Important occultists who were part of this group included Aleister Crowley, Arthur Waite, Pamela Coleman Smith, etc. Pamela Smith and Arthur Waite created the Rider-Waite (also called Rider-Waite-Smith) deck in 1909. Smith's illustrations for the deck were greatly inspired by the Sola Busca artwork, the earliest known tarot card deck dating back to the 15th century.

The Rider-Waite deck.
https://www.pexels.com/photo/tarot-cards-13321546/

Also, Smith was the first to use images, human figures, and other symbols for the Minor Arcana cards, which were, until then, represented by a collection of swords, cups, pentacles, and coins. All these elements added by Pamela Smith made the Rider-Waite a trendy and sought-after deck when it was first released. It continues to rule in the tarot world even today.

The Rider-Waite-Smith deck is great for beginners. It uses situational images on the cards that anyone can easily relate to. The pictures on the cards of this deck are designed to spark and light up your intuition and trigger an emotional response in your brain, both of which help you connect the message received to the question asked.

Thoth

Lady Frieda Harris illustrated the Thoth or the Crowley Thoth tarot deck under the supervision of the famous occultist Aleister Crowley interlinked his own philosophy into the deck's images and symbolism. It has an Art Deco design, and the deck gets its name from Thoth, the Egyptian god of learning, writing, and reckoning.

The Thot deck.
https://www.maxpixel.net/Arcana-Spiritual-Esoteric-Tarot-Oracle-4140879

This deck is the second-most popular deck in use after the Rider-Waite deck. The best feature of the Thoth deck is that it is filled with stunning images and brilliant symbolism. The designs are unique and quite different from the traditional Rider-Waite deck. Crowley released his deck with a book called "The Book of Thoth." The book analyzes the tarot deck with Egyptian influences, the Tree of Life, Tetragrammaton, etc. Here are some of the differences between the Thoth and Rider-Waite decks:

The Rider-Waite deck's imagery, influenced by Christianity, Paganism, and the ideas and stories of the Medieval Era, is very intuitive, making it perfect for beginners. It is easy to learn quickly about the cards and their meanings. The images and symbolism of the Thoth deck are drawn from ancient esoteric occultism. Therefore, understanding and interpreting the cards' meanings takes some time and practice compared to the Rider-Waite. Usually, a more experienced practitioner would use the Thoth deck.

Some of the card names are different too. For example, the Strength card in the Rider-Waite deck is the Lust card in the Thoth deck. Also, the Suit of Pentacles in the Rider-Waite deck is the Suit of Disks in the Thoth deck. Similarly, there are some more differences between the two decks.

Marseille

The Tarot of Marseilles was very popular in France during the 17th and 18th centuries for playing. It is believed to have been created in Milan before its popularity and use spread to France, Northern Italy, and Switzerland. Like any standard tarot card deck, the Tarot of Marseilles or Tarot de Marseille also has 78 cards. With its amazing images and pictures, this deck first led tarot cards from being a mere playing deck to using it for occult purposes.

The tarot of Marseilles.
ttribution-ShareAlike 2.0 Generic (CC BY-SA 2.0) <https://creativecommons.org/licenses/by-sa/2.0/> https://www.flickr.com/photos/epist/15551700426

As a beginner, you should start with the Rider-Waite deck, learn and master the art of tarot card reading, and then perhaps you can move on to the other decks.

Modern-Day Uses of Tarot Cards

Today, tarot cards are used in multiple ways and are not restricted as a divination tool.

Tarot helps improve your mental health - Reading and using tarot cards are spiritual practices that help to strengthen mental and spiritual resolve. Reading tarot cards during stressful times is useful to improve your understanding of the current, difficult situation and also your responses and reactions to it.

Anxiety and depression are common mental ailments today, calling for the nurturing care of the affected person's soul. Tarot cards are very useful to this end. They improve your self-awareness which, in turn, helps you deal with the problems you are facing objectively. Tarot cards help you understand the undercurrents causing the problems in your life.

Tarot offers a holistic approach to any form of therapy - A genuine tarot card reader and practitioner will not hesitate to guide clients to counseling therapy and to qualified medical practitioners for help. However, Tarot offers a holistic approach to all kinds of therapy by helping clients open their hearts and minds to issues beyond conscious levels.

Tarot card readings help to spark therapeutic conversations - A tarot card specialist picks up cards. When a particular card is drawn, the client may see an interpretation that may or may not match what the tarot practitioner says. However, the consonance or dissonance in thoughts of the two helps clients to open up and spark therapeutic conversations.

To end this chapter on tarot basics, Mark Horn, the author of the bestselling book "Tarot and the Gates of Light: A Kabbalistic Path to Liberation," had this to say about the insights obtained from tarot cards, "*Tarot does not predict the future. However, the cards give you an amazingly clear picture of your present and the future so that you can make informed choices for optimal outcomes.*"

Chapter 2: Developing Your Psychic Powers First

The most important aspect of tarot card reading is the power of the reader's intuition. Psychic powers play a crucial role in accurate readings and interpretations of tarot card spreads, images, and drawings. Therefore, even before you pick up a deck, you must connect with, develop, and sharpen your psychic and/or intuitive powers.

It's important to sharpen your intuitive skills before attempting to read the cards.
https://unsplash.com/photos/D3SzBCAeMhQ

The Psychic Spectrum

Before moving on and explaining the psychic spectrum, it's a good idea to put aside some misconceptions about psychic or intuitive powers. Often, when people hear the word "psychic," their minds conjure up images of crystal balls. Sometimes, they think of neon-lit stores that lead to dark rooms in which an old woman sits with a crystal ball in front of her, a few animatronic contraptions to manipulate supernatural séances and experiences, fog machines, smoke screens, etc. Some have been trained to believe that the concept of "being a psychic" is a scam and that there is no truth in "extrasensory gifts."

The first step to tuning in to your psychic powers is to disconnect from these "scam" lessons that have been driven into human minds for years. Yes, there are frauds, con artists, and charlatans in the world of psychics, too, as there are in other industries and fields of work. These charlatans use fear or some other emotional blackmail to prey on vulnerable individuals. The book is not talking about such people when it speaks of "psychic powers."

A true psychic is someone with extrasensory gifts, meaning they can hear, see, feel, touch, and sense things and experiences beyond the physical world. A "normal" person may never be able to understand this ability with their thought process limited by the five senses. Most people are trained to recognize certain things in the physical world. For example, everyone knows the sky is blue or gray depending on the weather conditions. Many people can easily recognize happiness, sadness, anger, etc.

Human sensory experiences are all concretized into the material, tangible, or at least elements that they can easily feel. However, the deeper you try to dive into your sensory experiences, the more you'll realize that there are things you can sense that are not easily accessible to common people. When you keep diving deep into your "extrasensory powers," the more you will be able to access and harness the power of your psychic talent.

So, what is the ability to be a psychic? It is the ability to process sensory experiences and information at a deep spiritual, emotional, and mental level. A psychic could use both tangible and intangible stimuli. Of course, this definition is too narrow to cover the entire psychic spectrum because each of us is gifted with varying degrees of this talent. Therefore, the psychic spectrum is quite large and covers a lot right from small, seemingly insignificant sensory perceptions, like being able to sense cranky or angry moods in people, to much higher and subtler aspects that may appear magical to people with "normal" perception.

It may help to use an illustration to understand the concept of the psychic spectrum. Suppose four friends, Susan, Alia, Michael, and

Nathan, meet for dinner. Susan arrives first, unhesitatingly asks the lady at the reception for her reserved table, and is led there quickly. When she sits, Susan notices her plate does not have a spoon, and the one next to her is missing a fork. Her glass is filled with water. But the glass at the seat opposite her is empty. She sips from her glass and waits for her friends to arrive.

Next, Michael enters the hotel and notices the receptionist is busy on her phone. He hesitates, wondering if she is angry or sad about her situation. Michael is sensitive and doesn't want to break into her thoughts abruptly. So, he gently coughs to grab her attention. She looks up from her phone and smiles at Michael, who is relieved that she is okay. He is also led to the reserved table. He greets Susan, and they reminisce while Michael browses through the menu, wondering what he should eat.

Ali walks into the restaurant, and the sensory experiences she feels assault her. She observes the loud and garish decor of the place. Ali notices how efficiently and quickly the servers are doing their job. She hears a guest complaining loudly on the phone somewhere at the back. After putting the phone down, he snaps at the lady next to him and the two kids sitting on the opposite sofa. She wonders how long the lady and the children will accept his arrogant behavior. Will the children grow into aggressive or docile adults? Suddenly, she hears her name being called and notices Susan and Michael waving to her from a table. She hurries to join them.

Nathan walks in last, and his feelings and experiences are far more than any of his three friends. He is utterly overwhelmed by the sights, sounds, smells, movements, and, thanks to the jacked-up air conditioner, the coldness in the air. He can even sense the interpersonal dynamics of two couples sitting at two different tables. Out of the blue, he feels sadness hanging in the air as if the place had accumulated pain and agony. Nathan wondered if some kind of bad accident had happened. Maybe deaths? Or a fire that killed people? He meets his friends, and they have a good time together. But Nathan can't shake off the feeling of dread right through the meal.

From the above example, you can see that four different people saw and experienced different things in the same setting and amidst the same stimuli. Each person's sensory abilities and range are different and unique. Use this example to understand your own sensory abilities. How much stimuli and energy do you absorb? What kinds of stimuli affect you the most, spiritually, mentally, and/or emotionally? When you connect with your own gifts and talents, you can delve deep and harness your psychic power.

How to Develop Psychic Powers

More than not, psychic powers get maximum exposure during childhood. These talents are usually passed on by those who are close, such as family members or even dear friends. For example, a child's mother may be tuned in deeply to her psychic powers, and she could teach her child how to use them.

Children tend to observe and notice far more than adults because, at that stage, survival instincts are strong. As they grow older, they are trained to "not be so sensitive." They are taught not to believe in "absurd" things like ghosts and spiritual beings. They are conditioned into disconnecting themselves from their intuitive powers. They are taught that emotions and extrasensory elements are anathemas to scientific logic and reasoning.

It is time to turn the tables, accept your innate gifts, and know that psychic powers are not "strange and opposite" to science and logic but are merely outside the current purview of scientific metrics. Instead of suppressing your inherent gifts, you should embrace them and learn to develop them.

Treat your psychic powers as a long-lost friend. How do you see old buddies from school you've met after a long time? They are all new people now, right? They may seem like strangers at the beginning of the second innings. And yet, when you sit and talk with them, old memories lost in your subconscious mind will emerge, and those seemingly broken bonds will be formed again, stronger and better than before.

Do the same with your intuitive powers. Reconnect with it as you would a beloved childhood friend. Your intuition has always been part of your spirit. It is just that it lies forgotten in the debris of life complications. Dig it up and connect with it again. Use these daily exercises for help.

Colors with Emotions

Connect your emotions with colors. Here's an example. Suppose you have had a difficult conversation with your boss. You are angry that they don't seem to see your point of view. Associate anger with a color of choice, say brown. Every time you are angry, visualize the color brown filling your mind. When you do this repeatedly, your intuition will register the association of the color brown with anger, which, in turn, will help you see emotions that are not obvious.

For example, if you are having an apparently normal conversation with your spouse. But you see the color brown. Then it could mean that there is anger in the environment. And since you are not angry, it means your spouse is angry about something. You can speak to your spouse about it.

As another example, suppose someone was trying to flirt with you, and you liked the feeling. You can associate the feeling of romance and love with pink. Keep connecting this emotion with this color as much as you can. Soon, your intuition will associate pink with love and romance. After a while, if you see pink when your friend or a family member is talking about another person, your intuition is telling you there is a romantic link.

Room or Space Scanning

Scanning the environment or space around you is an excellent way to build your psychic abilities. This exercise might appear to be a wee bit awkward initially. However, no one else will see your practice because it is entirely in your mind. Use these steps to help you:

- Stand anywhere in the room or space you want to scan, ensuring you can see clearly on all sides.
- You can either move around physically for the scan or use your eyes.
- Note the sights, sounds, smells, objects, etc., in the space.
- Notice the corners, the windowsills, the doors and windows, tables and chairs, and all other furniture.
- What are the things that are most inviting to you?
- What are the things you don't like in the room?
- What objects are giving you a negative vibe?
- Which ones are giving you a positive vibe?

Make mental notes of your feelings about all these things. Remember to write them down before you forget them. Repeat the scanning exercise everywhere, including outside spaces such as parks, malls, offices, subways, etc. The scanning exercise will help you increase awareness of your surroundings. The more you develop this awareness, the better your chances of noticing energy shifts.

When you have mastered space or room scanning, extrapolate the exercise to past memories and experiences. Remember to recall as many details as possible about good and bad experiences. What created the shift in the energy that led to the pleasant or unpleasant experience?

The mastery of scanning your past memories will eventually help you foresee future events and happenings. Experts opine that this is one of the most basic but powerful exercises that leads to astral projection or the ability to have willful out-of-body experiences. Astral projection takes years of diligent and patient practice before anyone can concretize it. Only those with extremely powerful psychic abilities can do it. However, the scanning exercise mentioned above is the first step toward it.

Dream Journal

Dreams are a portal between the physical world and the spiritual world and otherworldly realms. They connect your subconscious and conscious minds. Dreams help you reach out to innumerable memories that are deeply embedded in your psyche. People constantly create boundaries between their conscious and subconscious minds in the physical world. These boundaries are needed because of their limited sensory abilities.

Here's how boundaries help you in the practical world. Every moment, your senses are assaulted by a range of stimuli, and you can't ingest all of them. You would go crazy if you had to do so. Most of your sensory experiences and memories go straight into your subconscious mind, where they are stored for later use if needed.

Dreams are the best ways to connect with your subconscious mind and retrieve those memories. A powerful connection with your subconscious mind helps develop your psychic abilities. And so, dreams are excellent pathways for improved intuitive powers.

Dreams happen in a world that is completely free of all constraints. You can move around effortlessly in your dreams without any physical barriers, anywhere and everywhere. You can travel to foreign lands. You can do time travel and go into the past and future.

Dreams are a representation of an alternative reality. The more you dream, the more powerful your intuition will become and the more comfortable you will be dealing with your subconscious mind. With this, you'll realize and harness the power of the fluidity that exists between worlds. Use these tips to start and maintain a dream journal:

- Always keep a pen and paper near your bed so that you can write down what you saw in your dreams as soon as you wake up. Immediacy and speed are key aspects of maintaining accurate dream journals. If you wake up in the middle of the night after a dream, try to jot down the points you can recall before going back to sleep.
- Use the present tense to write your dream journal. Write it as if you are in a dream. When you do this, the chances of recalling as many details as possible from your dream are high.
- Do not forget to add the emotions you felt. Not only is the plot or events that took place in the dream important, but also how you felt. Did you enjoy what happened? Or did it scare you or fill you with sadness? Did you feel shame or embarrassment? Was the setting familiar?

Dream journaling helps you create a strong connection with your subconscious mind and facilitates lucid dreaming, wherein you can navigate through and control your dream. Manifestation of desires can be used through lucid dreaming.

Reading the Energy of Objects and People

Everything in this cosmos is made up of energy. All tangible and intangible elements in the universe, including objects, people, feelings, thoughts, and all else, are energy manifestations in different forms. So, if you can read and interpret the energy of any element, you can uncover the hidden secrets that the element holds in its core which is a direct advantage to building your psychic powers.

First of all, find out if you are an energy sponge or a source of energy. Only when you know this can you take control of the energy in your vicinity. Most people are unaware of how their energy impacts others and the space around them. Some people's negative energies can blanket an entire room, and unexpectedly and inexplicably, the room's mood can transform from happy to sad.

In contrast, people with happy, positive vibes can spread joy and love to everyone in their vicinity. It is obviously ideal to avoid or counter negative vibes and positive vibes. Reading the energy of people and things will help you with this.

Use these tips to develop your energy reading skills:

Focus on body language - When trying to read people's energy, focus on nonverbal aspects as much as the words they say. Pay attention to their eyes, the tone of their voices, how they shake hands with you, and the vibes they give out.

Focus on your feelings and memories for objects - What kind of memories does an object evoke? Does it make you feel sad, happy, or angry? For example, if you had a ring with a heart made of stones to symbolize your ex-partner, and that relationship ended badly, leaving you heartbroken, any heart-shaped objects similar to that ring could evoke sadness or, perhaps, resentment in your mind. The energy from that object aligns with your feelings and thoughts.

Chapter 3: Kabbalah and Tarot: A Mystical Connection

Kabbalah mysticism can help the reader peer through the mysticism hidden in tarot cards. Life and the entire cosmos consist of complex layers of interconnected matter and energy. Kabbalah is the science that helps us understand and unravel this vast interconnectedness. Kabbalah is an eternal, timeless science that goes beyond the limited notions of time, space, and physical limitations that human beings are accustomed to.

Kabbalah is a Hebrew word that refers to the study of the universe's fundamental laws that support existence and non-existence. Importantly, although Kabbalah is a Hebrew word, the study of it is not limited to just one religious group. The concept of interconnectedness, the core belief of Kabbalah, is available in varying forms across various cultures and religions of the world.

For example, in Tibetan Buddhism, philosophical ideas similar to what is explained in Kabbalah are collectively called Kalachakra. Even modern physics, especially the discoveries of quantum physics, match the ideas mentioned in ancient Kabbalah texts. Yet, modern physics has a long way to go before it can "prove" what the wise ancients already knew and recorded.

The Tree of Life

According to Kabbalah, the Tree of Life consists of ten Sephirot (singular - Sephirah). The Tree of Life consists of the Three Triads, namely Intellect, Emotion, and Instinct Triads, laid out horizontally. These triads represent the flow of energy from the topmost, the Keter or Crown, which lies above the Intellect Triad, to the lowest Sephirah (the tenth one), the Malchut, beneath the Instinct Triad.

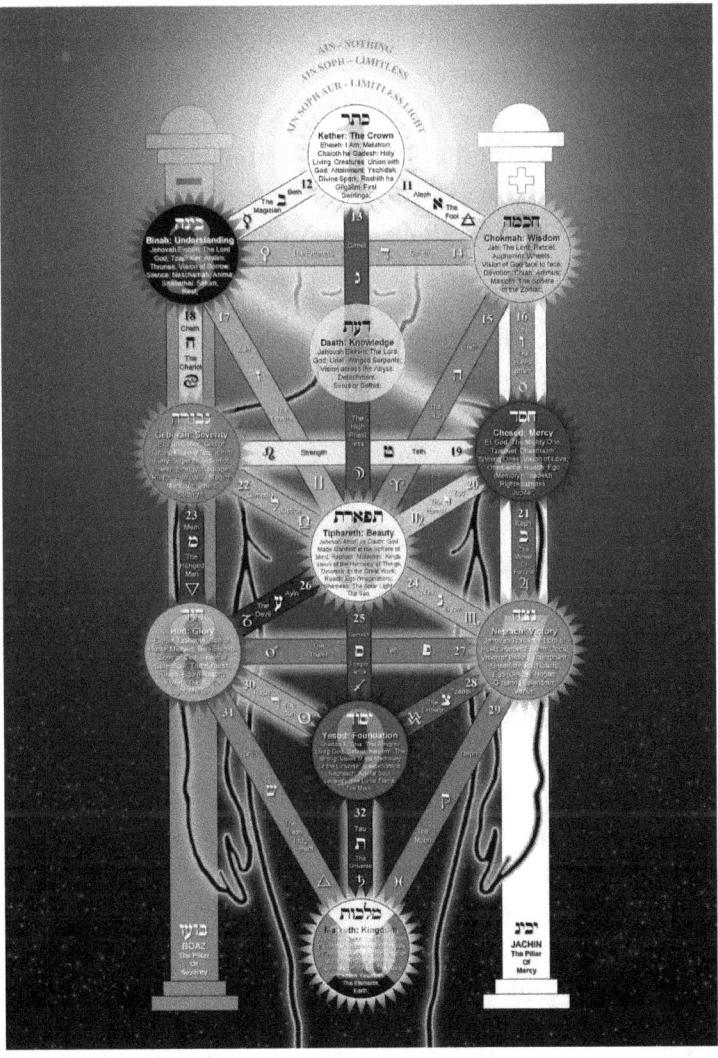

The Tree of Life.
Alan James Garner, CC BY-SA 3.0 <https://creativecommons.org/licenses/by-sa/3.0>, via Wikimedia Commons https://commons.wikimedia.org/wiki/File:Tree_of_Life_2009_large.png

Keter or the Crown is also called the "superconscious," an infinite field of energy and possibility. Keter is the ultimate state of being. It is the point touching the higher spiritual planes.

The energy flows through the Tree of Life and through each of the nine Sephirah until it reaches Malchut, representing the intention from the field of infinite possibilities to the space of finite manifestation.

The Intellect Triad

The Intellect Triad is the topmost rung in the Tree of Life and consists of the following three Sephiroth:

Chochmah - The Sephirah corresponds to the first seed of an idea drawn from Keter, the realm of infinite possibilities. The soul – the most ethereal aspect of the physical world, which conceives physical reality. Chochmah is referred to by many names, including inspiration, insight, inchoate awareness, etc., all of which point to that initial, almost imperceptible seed of thought that finds its way from the super consciousness into the topmost level of the consciousness.

Chochmah is the first flash of intellect or inspiration. It contains not only the seed of the idea but all the details as well. However, it is so concentrated that it appears only in its seed form while all else is obscured. The Chochmah is depicted as a dot containing all potential without actualization.

Binah - Binah is interpreted as understanding and refers to the state of the "seed idea" being fleshed out. It is the stage wherein the idea derived from the inspiration and insight of Chochmah gets a structure, and the story gets formulated. The color associated with Binah is dark red because it represents the color of congealed blood. In this context, blood is likened to the seed of an idea.

Binah also means to derive something from something else, to extract one thing about another. Binah expands and gives depth and breadth to the original seed of Chochmah. It is to be noted that Binah still only deals with the abstract potential contained in the idea.

Da'at - This Sephirah represents identifying with and connecting with the idea, structure, and associated story. The color of Da'at is gray because gray stands for intimate connection. Da'at is the Sephirah that enables abstract potential into actuality. The faculty of Da'at unites emotions and intellect. When you connect yourself with the idea so deeply that you become one with it, only then can you *feel for the idea* and get the power to bring it into actuality. This is the faculty of Da'at.

Emotion Triad

The fourth Sephirah is Chesed and is the first of the Emotion Triad. Chesed translates to unbounded love and mercy, which attracts and facilitates expansion, growth, widening the circle, and empathic concern. The color of Chesed is blue to symbolize the "flow," like the flow of blue water. Chesed is also referred to as loving-kindness, one that diffuses limitless compassion and benevolence.

Gevurah is the fifth Sephirah and the second in the Emotion Triad. It stands for strength and involves setting boundaries and limits, learning to say no, and finding focus. The color of Gevurah is red, the color that says "STOP" or "NO," which, in turn, means drawing limits or having limitations.

Gevurah is the attribute of control and restraint, concealing the infinite activating force of life and creation so that tangible entities can exist for human experience. Gevurah is also associated with law and justice so that Chesed or limitless kindness is distributed in a limited manner and according to one's merits. Gevurah's limits allow for creation and tangible reality to exist. Else, all and everything would have been nullified into the infinite Chesed.

Tiferet, the sixth Sephirah, stands for beauty and compassion. It stands for balancing and harmonizing opposing energies of all kinds. Tiferet's color is yellow, symbolizing the radiation of light. Tiferet harmoniously combines the faculties of Chesed and Gevurah, giving rise to beauty in the world. You can liken Tiferet to the heart in the center of your body, mediating between the right and left to create harmony and beauty.

Instinct Triad

Netzach is the seventh Sephirah and stands for victory. The word *Netzach* comes from "menatzeach," which means to "overcome" or "conquer." It represents the success of achieving your orchestrated intention after overcoming challenges and obstacles. The color of Netzach is purple, the color of dominance and power.

Hod is the next Sephirah in the Tree of Life. It represents surrender or submission, the exact opposite of the attributes of Netzach (overcoming and conquering). It tells you that letting go, giving in, and accepting are all ways of acknowledging what is beyond your control so that you can achieve your dreams. Orange, the color of hope and restoration, is the color of Hod.

Yesod is the last Sephirah of the Instinct Triad and represents twisting around and changing your truth until you find your authenticity. Yesod is the funnel through which the energy of the previous Sephiroth is channeled into the physical reality. The color of Yesod is green, which stands for renewal.

The last Sephirah is Malchut, the lowest one. It represents the culmination of the energy flow from Keter (the intangible superconsciousness) to the physical actuality. Malchut represents manifestation and expression. Its color is brown, the color of the earth and ground.

The Tree of Life is a map demonstrating the flow of intangible energy from infinite reality into tangible form. The Tree of Life urges us to find our deeper purpose and not merely get carried away by materialism. It tells you to dive deep and find the roots of your intangibles, which you can then harness into the physical world.

The Connection between Tarot and the Tree of Life

The Tree of Life represents the universal laws of reality. It stands for the eternal flow of the divine principle from the intangible realm into the physical reality governed by your five senses. The Tree of Life is not just somewhere out there; it lives in each individual. Your life is the microcosmic representation of the macrocosm. The echoes of the outside world are also found within you.

The flow of energy is upward as much as it is downward. If you follow the energy flow downward, you reach the physical manifestation of the intangible divine principle. If you follow it upward, you can find the divine source of infinite possibilities.

The 22 Paths of the Tree of Life and the Major Arcana

The Tree of Life consists of 10 Sephirot interconnected through 22 pathways, also called the Path of the Serpent. Each path connecting two nodes (or Sephirot) symbolizes the lessons you learn as you walk that path from one node to the connecting node.

The Path of the Serpent symbolizes a seeker's journey to reconnect with their lost divinity. The path represents the healing as one moves upward, longing to merge with the ultimate divine. The 22 pathways represent the growth and development as we walk through our internal world, similar to how the Major Arcana with 22 cards represents the Fool's Journey.

The Major Arcana symbolizes the evolution of the human spirit from ignorance to total enlightenment. It also represents the soul's return to its divine source, from matter back into spirit. The 22 cards of the Major Arcana are also related to the 22 Hebrew alphabets, namely Aleph, Beth, Gimel, Daleth, He, Vau, Zayin, Chet, Tet, Yod, Kaph, Lamed, Mem, Nun, Samech, Ayin, Phe, Tzaddi, Qoph, Resh, Shin, and Tav.

Here is a summary of the connections of the Major Arcana cards to their Hebrew and Kabbalah. As you learn more from the succeeding chapter, your understanding will get deeper and better.

The Fool's Card - Aleph - Primal Energy, unlettered, naive, and unaware. The Fool's Card represents the path between Keter and Chochmah.

The Magician Card - Beth - focus and attention to begin the journey toward learning and growth. It represents the path between Keter and Binah.

The High Priestess Card - Gimel - unconscious, uplifting. It stands for the path from Keter to Tiferet.

Empress Card - Daleth - nourishment, journey. It stands for the pathway from Chochmah to Binah.

Emperor Card - He - reasoning and vision - the path between Chochmah to Tiferet.

The Hierophant Card - Vau - Security, connections-path from Chochmah to Chesed.

The Lovers Card - Zayin - Cutting off, discernment, and the keen ability to distinguish accurately - the path from Binah to Tiferet.

The Chariot Card - Chet - Enclosure and separation - the path from Binah to Gevurah.

The Strength Card - Tet - twisting, surround - the path from Gevurah to Tiferet.

The Hermit Card - Yod - Work, action, and deeds - the path between Chesed and Tiferet.

The Wheel of Fortune Card - Kaph - grasp, hold, cover - the path between Chesed and Netzach.

The Justice Card - Lamed - Tongue, prod, dig - the path from Gevurah to Chesed.

The Hanged Man - Mem - Reversal, change over, overpower - Gevurah to Hod path.

The Death Card - Nun - Activity, life, revival, sprouting - Tiferet to Netzach path.

The Temperance Card - Samech - Principle, doctrine, support system - Tiferet to Yesod pathway.

The Devil Card - Ayin - Knowledge, lessons and skills, experience - Tiferet to Hod pathway.

The Tower Card - Phe - Words, speech, communication - Hod to Netzach pathway.

The Star Card - Tzaddi - Harvesting, fruition, integrity - Netzach to Yesod pathway.

The Moon Card - Quoph - Unseen, not obvious, hidden - Netzach to Malchut pathway.

The Sun Card - Resh - Redeeming, ultimate, finest - from Hod to Yesod.

The Judgment Card - Shin - Destruction, consume - from Hod to Malchut.

The World Card - Tav - The ultimate truth, covenant - from Yesod to Malchut.

Chapter 4: The Astrology behind Tarot

This chapter is dedicated to the astrological perspective of tarot cards. It will begin with enhancing your understanding of astrology.

What Is Astrology?

Astrology can be called "the language of the sky." It studies the movements of planets and stars and how they affect human life. It is the study of the connection between human events and celestial activity.

Astrology looks into the movement and patterns of stars and how they affect human life.
ESA/Hubble, CC BY 4.0 <https://creativecommons.org/licenses/by/4.0>, via Wikimedia Commons https://commons.wikimedia.org/wiki/File:A_home_for_old_stars.jpg

Celestial activities include the movement of the planets, stars, and zodiac signs. Human events include careers, relationships, achievements of dreams, and everything else humans desire. An astrologer practices astrology. There are multiple benefits of consulting an astrologer.

An astrologer can predict your future. This does not mean that you'll know the exact future outcomes. Based on the celestial activity, your astrologer can give you significant insights into your future. Nor can you really change your future. However, if the future is expected to be not-so-pleasant, then you can prepare yourself to make the best of it. If great things are expected, you can prepare to optimize the results as much as possible.

You can check your relationship compatibility. Strong relationships are formed between individuals whose thought processes and life expectations align more or less with each other. When your and your partner's physical, mental, and spiritual compatibilities are aligned, the chances of your relationship sustaining and growing from strength to strength are high. Astrology helps you with partner compatibility checks.

You can counter challenges and obstacles with the help of astrology. Astrologers can help you break down seemingly insurmountable obstacles and challenges into smaller, manageable portions by helping you deal with them one small problem at a time, based on celestial activity. You can learn about challenges waiting around the corner and prepare yourself to deal with them.

Planets and Their Significance

Different planets and other celestial bodies are connected to various aspects of human personality. The position of planets on your birth chart and their movements around your zodiac impacts your personality, how you think, and how you act and respond. Interpreting the significance of planets and their movements helps predict your future and understand your past and present.

Now, look at the connections between the seven planets according to western astrology: the sun, moon, Mercury, Venus, Mars, Saturn, and Jupiter.

The Sun - The Sun symbolizes the self and is the light of life on the earth. The Sun is associated with masculinity, creativity, self-expression, ego, vitality, and individuality. This planet represents a father figure, power, confidence, and authority. The position of the Sun on your birth chart determines how you deal with people. In a strong position, the Sun endows you with willpower and life-giving energy. It also represents your connection with your spiritual nature and your higher self. The Sun takes one month to move from one zodiac to another.

The Moon is the planet of emotions and is associated with personality traits like habits, behaviors, instincts, intuition, and femininity. It takes 2-3 days to move from one zodiac to the next. The Moon symbolizes your soul and your inner self. In a difficult position, the Moon can influence your moods and stability of mind negatively. The Moon makes you strong, courageous, and calm when placed in the ascendant house.

Mercury - Mercury deals with communication, ideas, and intelligence. It takes 3-4 weeks to move between zodiacs. Mercury rules over analytical skills, responsive and reactionary abilities, grasping and memory powers, and verbal and nonverbal communication. When Mercury is in the right place in your birth chart, your mental strength is great, and your ability to communicate is also very good.

Venus - Venus is the planet of beauty and rules over human activities such as love, relationships, pleasure, and art. Transiting from one zodiac to the next takes about 4-5 weeks. This planet of beauty symbolizes your love language and aesthetics. In your horoscope, Venus governs your personal taste, courtships, and relationships (both with people and finances).

Mars is the planet of action and takes about 6-7 weeks to transit between zodiac signs. It governs passion, aggression, libido, courage, desire, and competition. Mars rules over your determination and drive to get things done. The position of Mars in your life gives you insights into your energy, sexuality, and the dreams and desires that light you up. It also rules over your anger and, in a difficult position, can make your anger your biggest enemy.

Jupiter is the planet of expansion and is associated with wisdom, optimism, growth, property, and influence. It takes about 12-13 months to transit between zodiac signs; Jupiter showers you with luck, prosperity, health, and all the good things in life, provided it is in the right place in your horoscope.

Saturn is the planet of structure and governs karma, discipline, perseverance, obstacles, restriction, law, and justice. It is the slowest moving planet in astrology and takes about 2-3 years to transit between zodiac signs. Saturn is all about moral authority and obligations. When

Saturn impacts your life negatively (seemingly), it is a reminder that you need to handle your responsibilities and duties better, create boundaries for your safety, and know your karma is coming around.

Understanding the Zodiac

In addition to the planets, astrology is governed by the 12 zodiac signs (according to date of birth), which include:

- Aries (March 21 - April 19)
- Taurus (April 20 - May 20)
- Gemini (May 20 - June 20)
- Cancer (June 21 - July 22)
- Leo (July 23 - August 22)
- Virgo (August 23 - September 22)
- Libra (September 23 - October 22)
- Scorpio (October 23 - November 21)
- Sagittarius (November 22 - December 21)
- Capricorn (December 22 - January 19)
- Aquarius (January 20 - February 18)
- Pisces (February 19 - March 20).

Each zodiac sign mentioned above has a place in this cosmos; none is good or bad. They work together to render karmic outcomes. The 12 zodiac signs are categorized into four groups according to the four elements resulting in four types, namely fire signs, water signs, air signs, and earth signs.

Water signs, including Cancer, Scorpio, and Pisces, tend to be overly sensitive and emotional. They have powerful intuition, can be mysterious too, and rarely do anything garrulous. They thrive on intimacy and quiet, deep conversations.

Fire signs (Aries, Leo, and Sagittarius) are usually very temperamental and passionate, quick to anger, but equally easy to forgive and move on. They have abundant energy and are always on the lookout for adventure and ever-ready for action! Like the element they represent, they are very strong and inspire others to be their best.

Earth signs (Taurus, Virgo, and Capricorn) are not only grounded themselves but also keep the others downright practical and grounded. They tend to have realistic perspectives but can be quite emotional too. They are deeply connected to materialistic things, perhaps due to their deep sense of practicality and logic.

Air signs (Gemini, Libra, and Aquarius) tend to be highly talkative and enjoy social interactions. They are also very rational and deep thinkers who analyze everything through their sharp intellects. They are book lovers who enjoy philosophical discussions. And yet, people born under the earth signs can also be quite superficial.

Now take a look at the characteristics of people born under each of the 12 signs.

Aries - The symbol of Aries is the head of a ram. Like the ram, people born under this sign are fiery (apropos to the fire element) and love competition. They dive first into all kinds of competition, often impetuously. Patience is not one of their virtues, but outright (even painful sometimes) honesty is. Like Mars, which rules over Aries, the people born under this zodiac are highly driven and always want to come first in everything they do.

Taurus - The bull's head represents this earth sign. Taureans love to relax in calm, peaceful surroundings. Like the bull, they love to soak for hours in water. They are persistent and loyal though they are often stereotyped for laziness and bullheadedness. Taurus is ruled by Venus, the planet of love, which makes Taureans one of the most sensual people.

Gemini - The symbol of this air sign is the celestial twins (sometimes, the Roman numeral II), and rightly so. They are so ambitious and want so many things that they are happy to lead two lives to achieve their dreams. Like the double life they like to lead, people born under Gemini are known to be as sociable and intelligent as indecisive and superficial. Mercury rules over this zodiac sign, so Geminis can absorb and process information faster than most people.

Cancer - Crab is the Cancer zodiac symbol. People born under this water sign are great at managing their emotional and materialistic realms with equal elan. Cancerians are charitable and friendly people. And yet, they can get crabbily and hurtfully blunt if you try to bring them out of their shells (or comfort zones). They are highly intuitive people and emotional sponges and will go to any lengths to protect themselves emotionally. Cancer is ruled by the Moon, which explains their highly emotional personality.

Leo - The lion is the symbol of Leo. Like the king of the jungle, Leos are loyal and passionate. Still, they can also be highly dramatic about everything involving them and enjoy basking in their own glory. Like the Sun that rules this sign, people born under this fire sign do not shy away from embracing their royal status. They manifest it through vivacity and their fiery attitude. While they are proud and brave, they tend to be highly aggressive and arrogant.

Virgo - This earth sign is symbolized by the Maiden, who represents the goddess of wheat and agriculture. Virgo is ruled by Mercury, the one who handles communication. Virgos are diligent, practical, logical, organized, and deeply connected with the practical world. They know how to get things done and done well. Their biggest drawback and strength is perfectionism. So, they are diligent in improving their skills and also end up worrying more than needed.

Libra - The balance scale represents this air sign. Librans are highly fixated on achieving equilibrium in every situation. Obsessed with symmetry, Librans chase balance wherever they go, especially in matters of the heart (which is not necessarily easy). They are known to be clever extroverts but hate being put in situations where they have to make hard decisions. Venus is their ruling planet.

Scorpio - People born under this water sign use emotional energy as their fuel to seek wisdom both from physical and spiritual realms. Scorpios (symbol is scorpion) tend to be powerful psychics making them appear elusive and mysterious. Thanks to their complicated and dynamic personalities, Scorpios are one of the most misunderstood zodiac signs. Mars rules over Scorpio, from whom they get their passion and aggression. If they have a cause to fight for, they are relentless and unstoppable, and no fear can hinder them in their path of achieving what they want.

Sagittarius - The adventurous Sagittarians love to travel everywhere in every form (physical, emotional, and spiritual journeys) in search of knowledge and wisdom, symbolic of blazing arrows. People born under this fire sign are extroverts; their enthusiasm and zest for life are infectious. Ruled by Jupiter, Sagittarians' great humor and intense curiosity make them winners in all their endeavors. Their biggest weakness is the absence of tact and diplomacy when dealing with the outside world and with people who are different from themselves.

Capricorn - The symbol of this earth sign is a mythological creature with a fish's tail and a goat's body. Patience, dedication, and perseverance are the hallmarks of the people born under this sign. This sign symbolizes dedication, responsibility, and time. Capricorns value tradition and are quite serious in their outlook. They make great leaders and can make solid, realistic, and well-executable plans.

Aquarius - Aquarius is a water sign, and people born under this sign are revolutionaries and highly progressive. The symbol of Aquarius is a water bearer, the harbinger of the source of life, water. Aquarians are dedicated to making this world a better place. They strive for the welfare of society and the world. They are deep thinkers who, although quite shy and reserved, do not hesitate to fight for a righteous cause. Saturn is the ruler of Aquarius.

Pisces - Symbolized by two fishes swimming toward each other in opposing directions, it reflects the dichotomous and conflicting perspectives that Pisceans tend to have between reality and fantasy. Being the last sign in the zodiac, it is as if Pisces has absorbed all the lessons taught by the previous 11 signs, thereby making Pisceans the most intuitive, wise, and empathetic person in the world. Ruled by Jupiter, people born under this water sign are friendly, selfless, and always ready to give a helping hand to those in need.

The Connection between Astrology and Tarot

Astrology and tarot are so closely connected that a combined form of predictive reading called *tarotscope* is very popular. Tarotscope is the art of reading an individual's horoscope through tarot cards. It is interesting to see how astrology and tarot are associated with each.

- Each of the 12 zodiac signs is associated with a Major Arcana card.
- Each number card in the Minor Arcana card is also associated with a zodiac sign.
- The court cards and aces are connected through the four elements, which, in turn, are connected to the 12 zodiacs.
- The Suit of Wands is associated with the fire element and, therefore, the three fire signs: Aries, Leo, and Sagittarius.

- The Suit of Cups is associated with the water element and, therefore, is connected to the three water signs Cancer, Scorpio, and Pisces.
- The Suit of Swords is associated with the Air element and, therefore, with the three air signs Gemini, Libra, and Aquarius.
- The Suit of Pentacles is associated with the earth element and, therefore, with the three earth signs Taurus, Virgo, and Capricorn.

The associations of the Major Arcana cards, the 12 zodiac signs, and the planets are as follows:

- The Sun is Leo's ruler and is associated with the Sun card
- The Moon is Cancer's ruler and is associated with the High Priestess card
- Mercury, the ruler of Gemini and Virgo, is connected to the Magician card
- Venus, the ruler of Libra and Taurus, is associated with the Empress card
- Mars, the ruler of Scorpio and Aries, is associated with the Tower card
- Jupiter, the ruler of Pisces and Sagittarius, is associated with the Wheel of Fortune card
- Saturn, the ruler of Aquarius and Capricorn, is associated with the World card
- Aries is associated with the Emperor card
- Taurus is associated with the Hierophant card
- Gemini is associated with the Lovers' card
- Cancer is associated with the Chariot card
- Leo is associated with the Strength card
- Virgo is associated with the Hermit card
- Libra is associated with the Justice card
- Scorpio is associated with the Death card
- Sagittarius is associated with the Temperance card
- Capricorn is associated with the Devil card

- Aquarius is associated with the Star card
- Pisces is associated with the Moon card
- Cards 2, 3, and 4 (of all four suits) are associated with the cardinal signs: Aries, Cancer, Libra, and Capricorn
- Cards 5, 6, and 7 (of all four suits) are linked with the fixed signs, namely Taurus, Leo, Scorpio, and Aquarius
- Cards 8, 9, and 10 (of all four suits) are associated with mutable signs, namely Gemini, Virgo, Sagittarius, and Pisces

Combine all of the above connections and interconnections, and your tarot card reading will become more accurate, thanks to lateral associations with the elements of other equally powerful and popular predictive and divination tools.

Chapter 5: The Cards and Numerology

Tarot card reading is not just about memorizing what each of the 78 cards signifies. It includes multiple layers of understanding with direct and indirect connections with the querent's life and questions. Like Kabbalah and astrology, numerology is another useful tool for accurate and personalized interpretations of tarot cards. This section of tarot card reading is called Tarot Numerology. It will start by explaining the concept of numerology.

Understanding Numerology

What is numerology? Pythagoras, the ancient Greek mathematician, believed that, like other things in this universe, numbers are also endowed with energetic vibrations. And this is the basis for developing numerology as a divination, healing, and predictive tool.

Numerology is the study of numbers and how their energetic vibrations impact our lives. Every human is born with an inherent set of numbers imbibed into their personality or psyche. These numbers hold secrets and truths about people and indicate their life paths, challenges, and successes. Single-digit numbers from 0-9 form the foundational building blocks of numerology.

The most significant number that is part of every human is their Life Path Number based on the date of birth. This remains unchanged throughout an individual's life, greatly influencing your personality and how you live your life. Life Path Numbers show the challenges and opportunities you can get in your life. They reveal secrets about your personality that remain hidden deep in your psyche. Connecting with your Life Path Number will help you connect with your authentic self, which, in turn, will help you lead an authentic life instead of one driven by external stimuli.

Life Path Numbers

Before explaining what each Life Path Number represents and signifies, here is an illustration of how you calculate your Life Path Number. Suppose your birthdate is October 1, 1970. Begin by reducing each of your birthdate components into single digits.

The month is October which is 10 - 1+0 = 1

The date is 01, which remains = 1

Year is 1970 - 1+9+7+0 = 17 which is again reduced to (1+7) = 8

Then, add all the final signal digit numbers (1+1+8) = 10

And again, reduce this to 10 (1+0) = 1

So, your Life Path Number is 1.

1 - Number 1 is related to Aries, the first zodiac sign. People whose Life Path Number is 1 tend to be excellent leaders and innovators. The power of Aries' motivation drives them to become pioneers. Considering their outstanding leadership skills, the Ones tend to be very lonely people as they are most often found at the top of the ladder, strong but isolated and alone.

Conversely, their inherent desire for excellence can make them bossy, stubborn, and arrogant. They forget that no one lives on an island. You need support from other people. Playing second fiddle in any given situation is a huge challenge for Ones.

2 - Twos make excellent mediators and facilitators. The number 2 is connected with harmony, unity, and balance. The Twos can bring peace in a dissonant environment filled with friction and disharmony. Twos have powerful intuitions and can detect subtle energy shifts in any given environment, giving them the advantage of nipping the problem in the bud before it magnifies uncontrollably.

On the flip side, because Twos are so tuned in to harmony and balance, they find it very difficult to deal with frictions and conflicts and, therefore, end up under-appreciated. People often mistake Twos' compassion for weakness. This can be countered if Twos cease to seek external validation.

3 - Three is the expansion, growth, and fertility within a protected structure and/or framework to allow for growth and development without losing out to unbridled, dangerous freedom. People with 3 as their Life Path Number generally tend to have a positive, youthful outlook on life. They are zesty and love interacting with people, thanks to their excellent creative expression.

4 - In numerology, the number 4 stands for strength and efficiency. Interestingly, 4 is a much-feared number (1 3 adds up to 4). However, in truth, the number 4 carries wisdom and rationality on its head. It is a number that tells you to use your head rather than your heart to move forward. It is known to render stability and grounding in any concerned situation or for the concerned person. It also symbolized advancements but through the tried and tested traditional methods and not by anything new.

5 - "Curiosity killed the cat" is quite the opposite of the key characteristic of the number 5 in numerology. This number is driven by curiosity. People with 5 as their Life Path Number tend to be so curious to experience a variety of experiences in life to feel fulfilled. They crave adventure and freedom; the only goal they know to set is to get out there and experiment and experience. They are highly adaptable people and can fit into any kind of environment. On the flip side, Fives can be quite unreliable and non-committal.

6 - Number 6 represents the heart. It stands for unconditional support and love. People born with 6 as their Life Path Number are usually great nurturers and healers. They are highly empathetic and, in a group, are usually seen as harbingers of light and hope. They are great at letting others open up their hearts to them. They can be great friends and lovers. Conversely, the Sixes tend to be overly sacrificing and idealistic. When, practically, these things cease to work after a while, they tend to get resentful and angry.

7 - The number 7 stands for depth and is a number that does not deal with anything frivolous. People born with this Life Path Number tend to know that scratching the surface is not enough. You need to dig deep everywhere because gold is always buried deep. Therefore, the Sevens are always asking questions, finding more answers, doing relentless research, and using all their senses to collect as much information as they can. Conversely, Sevens can be quite reclusive and secretive as they spend most of their time analyzing, researching, and digging deeper.

8 - Number 8 symbolizes achievements measured and tracked by the goals reached. People with 8 as their Life Path Number have a strong drive for success. They are highly ambitious and will work hard to realize their dreams only to dream more. Their primary goal is to achieve, and the best part is even during down periods, they find the strength to keep striving towards their goals. On the flip side, Eights can have a materialistic outlook with a bossy attitude.

9 - Nine in numerology stands for completion, or the ending of one cycle and the start of a new one. This number ushers a period of change and transformation. People born with this Life Path Number tend to be highly tolerant and spiritually awakened. They handle the pain with grace and dignity. They are highly supportive people too. On the flip side, Nines tend to indulge in excessive self-sacrifice leading to resentment and needless suffering.

Master Numbers

Certain numbers should not be reduced further into single-digit numbers. These are called Master Numbers and include 11, 22, and 33. People born under the aegis of these Master Numbers are believed to turn out very influential and successful. There is something very powerful about these three numbers that tend to heighten the person's potential to actualize their intuitive, intellectual, and materialistic goals.

11 - Number 11 in numerology is directly connected to intuition and the higher planes of wisdom. People born with 11 as their Life Path Number tend to be associated with their single-digit counterparts, namely 2 (1+1). Therefore, Elevens are also associated with harmony and empathy though they feel it far more deeply than the Twos. Also, Elevens share a few attributes of Ones, such as innovativeness and the desire to make a difference. On the flip side, Elevens can be quite overwhelmed by their empathetic nature, leading them to stress and depression, even self-doubt.

22 - Master Number 22 conjoins spirituality and materialism. The Twenty-Twos are endowed with the ability to receive profound insights and use them for the greater good. The single-digit companion of 22 is 4, the number associated with practicality and dedication.

Dedication is one of the biggest discerning elements that separate the Twenty-Twos from others. Hard work is deeply ingrained in their genetic and mental makeup. This dedication serves their personal purpose of achieving their goals and dreams and helpful attitudes toward humankind. They are continuously looking for ways to improve the lives of others.

On the flip side, because they are so hardworking and dedicated, they don't like to use up their energy for seemingly frivolous things such as emotions and the like making them seem like the "all work, no play" kind of people, which can be a big put off.

33 - Having a Life Path Number of 33 is very rare as it requires an uncommon combination of date of birth to get this. But those who have it become great healers and spiritual leaders. They become Master Teachers. They are selfless, often never thinking of themselves and always putting others before themselves. Altruism is deeply embedded in their psyche. Therefore, one of the biggest lessons that Thirty-Threes can learn is to keep themselves healed and happy so that they can be available for the amazing amount of good they can give to this world.

FAQs on Tarot Numerology

Why is numerology important in tarot reading? There are multiple reasons, some of which are shown below:

- If a number tarot card appears repeatedly, then there could be a strong indication of the numerical significance of that number rather than just the tarot card's meaning. Often, numbers appearing repeated in tarot card spreads represent the time or duration of an event or a situation.
- Suppose there are sequential numbers in a tarot card draw. In that case, it could indicate the start and the end period of an event, issue, or experience.
- Numerology gives additional nuances to tarot card spreads for more insightful and accurate readings than alone.

Here are some FAQs to help you understand better.

Q. What is the meaning of drawing an Ace in a tarot reading?

A. In tarot, the number 1 (or Aces) symbolizes the start of a journey. It tells you that everything is happening to facilitate the beginning of a new venture or journey for you. If you draw an Ace, it could signify the germination of a new idea or opportunity. An Ace in reverse (upside-down to the tarot reader and right-side-up facing the receiver) could mean that a great idea is there but is being blocked.

Q. What is the meaning of drawing Two in tarot?

A. Drawing a Two could represent the conjunction of two opposing forces to bring balance and harmony. Like the Twos who are always thinking of harmonizing environments of conflicts, drawing a Two could signify cooperating partnerships.

Q. What is the meaning of drawing Two in reverse?

A. If you draw a Two in reverse, it could indicate imbalance and disharmony in the concerned situation or relationship.

Q. What is the meaning of drawing Three in tarot?

A. Three stands for expression and growth. Drawing a three could indicate the end of one venture or phase and the preparation to begin the next one. As this number also stands for growth, it means you have achieved growth and progress in the previous phase and that you are moving toward your ultimate goal.

Q. What is the meaning of drawing Three in reverse?

A. In reverse, the Three card could indicate a time of self-isolation for self-improvement. Also, three stands for groups too. Therefore, a reverse three could mean it is time for you to stand alone, away from groups.

Q. What does 4 symbolize in tarot?

A. Four stands for stability, grounding, manifestations, and foundations. Drawing a Four card could indicate that your desires and dreams are being materialized or manifested. Four is a good sign for the Law of Attraction. But it does not mean that it is a period of sitting back and relaxing, thinking that all work is done. Work has to continue.

Q. What is the meaning of 4 in reverse?

A. Drawing a Four card in reverse could indicate a situation or person that lacks stability and grounding.

Q. What is the meaning of drawing a Five card?

A. In tarot, Five symbolizes instability and change, both of which might be unpleasant but necessary for growth. When you draw a Five card, it could indicate an upcoming change in dynamics or situation.

Q. What is the meaning of drawing a reverse Five?

A. If you draw a Five card in reverse, it could indicate a reluctance or resistance to face an upcoming, important challenge or obstacle that has a high chance of leading you to growth and development.

Q. What is the meaning of drawing a Six card?

A. In tarot, drawing a Six means it is a time for resting and healing. It indicates a time for harmony and cooperation.

Q. What is the meaning of drawing a reverse Six?

A. A reverse Six could indicate a time of imbalance and disharmony.

Q. What is the meaning of drawing a Seven?

A. In tarot, drawing a Seven usually means a time to reflect and assess before proceeding further.

Q. What is the meaning of drawing a reverse Seven?

A. A reverse Seven could mean a lack of clarity or focus or an overwhelming amount of confusing options.

Q. What is the meaning of drawing an Eight card?

A. In tarot, Eight represents accomplishment and mastery. Like the infinity symbol, 8 represents eternal motion and flow. If you draw an Eight, it could indicate the need for continuous striving and work to achieve the desired goals.

Q. What is the meaning of drawing a reverse Eight?

A. Drawing an Eight in reverse could indicate the lack of hard work to achieve desired results and/or the absence of material success.

Q. What is the meaning of drawing a Nine card?

A. In tarot, drawing a Nine could indicate fulfillment and completion. It means the rewards of hard work can be expected.

Q. What is the meaning of drawing a reverse Nine?

A. Drawing a reverse Nine could indicate a lack of fulfillment and closure.

Chapter 6: Meet the Cards I: Major Arcana

It's now time to take a closer look at each of the cards in the tarot deck. The chapter starts with the 22 cards of the Major Arcana. Let's dive right in.

The Fool

The Major Arcana begins with the Fool, a metaphor for naivety and innocence. This card represents each person in their life journey as they start with innocent faith and take their first step eagerly despite knowing that the journey is rife with struggles and obstacles. The Fool's card represents the beginning, a fresh and spontaneous beginning. The Fool depicted on the card with his arms flailing wide and his head held high with hopes is a symbol of a simple soul ready to embrace everything that comes his way.

The fool.
https://pixabay.com/es/illustrations/el-tonto-tarot-tarjeta-magia-6016940/

The Fool stands at the edge of a cliff but is totally oblivious to the dangers ahead. He is completely unaware of all the dangers and hazards that the journey has in store for him. He is just totally happy to take what comes his way. The Fool is more or less outside the other cards of the Major Arcana and is like the number 0, which stands in the middle of positive and negative integers. Like zero, the Fool represents nothingness or emptiness and gets filled with desires and feelings as he undertakes his journey.

The Fool's card represents the entire cosmos and all the planets and zodiac signs because he stands for nothingness which holds everything. In the concept of a journey, the Fool stands for the conception of an idea or thought. The keywords of this air tarot card are innocence, free-spiritedness, risk-taking, and adventure.

The Fool is the first path between Keter and Chochmah. Keter or the Crown is Pure Spirit and is symbolized by a mere point but one that has infinite potential. However, it embodies everything in this cosmos. Keter needs to act for the process of creation to begin. So, Keter moves forward and thrusts itself on Chochmah (or Wisdom).

In the same way, the Fool represents infinite potential. This card is the first step that the soul has taken toward entering the cosmos from Nothing (or Zero) to something. The Fool's path represents the complex transformation of 0 to 1 or something, which is the beginning of the tangible universe.

Drawing an upright Fool usually indicates the start of a new journey. During this time, you are likely to feel euphoric and excited without any constraint. If you draw a reverse Fool card, it could indicate a time of danger wherein an action is taken without considering the consequences. It could also mean that you are living in the moment without any plans for the future, which may be a good or bad thing.

The Magician

The second of the 22 Major Arcana cards is depicted with a magician who represents the positive and masculine side of creativity. The Magician represents conscious awareness, a force that empowers people to create through the sheer use of willpower.

The magician.
https://pixabay.com/es/illustrations/el-mago-cartas-de-tarot-tarot-mago-6103696/

The Magician's right-hand points upward to the sky. His left hand is turned downward, facing the earth. This symbolism translates to "As above, so below," a phrase pregnant with multiple meanings, including the following:

- Earth is a reflection of heaven
- The external world is a reflection of our inner world
- The microcosm is a reflection of the macrocosm

The Magician also indicates that he can mediate between the tangible and intangible worlds. On his table are the four suits of the Minor Arcana, each representing the four elements, fire, air, water, and earth. Therefore, the Magician is a master of all four elements. The infinity symbol hovering above his head represents the infinite possibilities when one's will and spirit are strong.

This card represents the Number 1, which symbolizes unity. So, the Magician is adept at his craft and a student continuously seeking lessons from the world. The power of the Magician is knowledge, and he is a relentless seeker of this power. He indicates that magic happens when you can bend your will to realize your intangible dreams into tangible outcomes and goals.

The keywords associated with the Magician card are desire, willpower, concentration, focus, and the manifestation of desire through skills and knowledge. Drawing an upright Magician card could indicate that you are ready to achieve your fullest potential, and it is time to delve deep into your willpower and make things happen. If you get a Magician card, it means you must not hold back anywhere lest you let go of opportunities that come knocking on your doors.

In reverse, the Magician card could indicate wasted talent, manipulation, cunningness, deception, and trickery. Drawing a Magician card in reverse could indicate a time of care and caution because you could be lured by deception and illusion. All may not seem as is, and it could be that someone is trying to manipulate you into a trap.

The Magician is associated with Mercury, which rules over Gemini and Virgo. In the process of creativity, the Magician card represents incubation, wherein the idea is slowly but steadily finding ways to concretize in the tangible world. It is connected to the air element. In Kabbalah, the Magician card is the path between Keter and Binah and indicates the start of material production. The Magician is the director of channeled energy.

The High Priestess

The keywords for an upright High Priestess card include intuition, mystery, inner voice, spirituality, unconscious mind, and powers associated with the higher planes of consciousness. In reverse, the Empress card implies hidden motives, superficiality, repressed intuition, and confusion.

The high priestess.
https://pixabay.com/es/illustrations/tarot-cartas-de-tarot-magia-fortuna-6246912/

The High Priestess is depicted as sitting on a cube-shaped stone placed between two pillars. In addition to symbolizing the female-male, good-evil duality in nature, these two pillars symbolize Jachin, the Pillar of Establishment, and Boaz, the Pillar of Strength associated with the Temple of Solomon.

That she sits between the two pillars signifies her mediatory skills through which she maintains the balance between two opposing forces.

Suppose you draw an Empress card in your tarot reading. In that case, it indicates listening to your intuition and not only relying on your intellect to get things done. In fact, drawing an Empress card should compel you to put your intuition above your intellect in the given situation. It indicates using mediation, prayers, and spiritual work for the concerned query.

When the High Priestess comes into your reading, it means she is calling you to listen to what she says, trust her, and follow her into the balanced world of opposing forces that might seem frightening initially. Still, it will lead you to great success and happiness. She is calling upon you to seek answers within yourself.

If you draw a reversed High Priestess card, it could indicate that you find it difficult to listen to your intuition. It tells you that you have been ignoring your instincts and need to reconnect with them in new ways because the "rational" approach will not work for the current situation. A reverse High Priestess indicates that you must not be afraid to ask yourself pertinent and difficult questions so that new paths to your intuitive powers can be lit to find your way in the dark.

Interestingly, the Fool meets both the Magician and High Priestess almost immediately at the start of his journey. These two cards balance each other, the Magician's positive, active, masculine elements with the High Priestess's negative, mysterious, feminine elements. It is important to know positive and negative do not have a "good" or "bad" meaning in tarot. They are merely opposite but of equal value and stature. Both positive and negative are imperative elements for balance and structure in this world.

The High Priestess is associated with the Moon and is, therefore, connected with the water signs, namely Pisces, Cancer, and Virgo. In Kabbalah, she is the path that connects Keter to Tiferet, the path connecting the Pure Spirit to beauty and harmony. The name of this path is gimel which means "camel," the self-sustaining animal of the desert that can survive for days on end without water. In the same way, the High Priestess can draw energy from the depths of her being to harness a huge reservoir of self-confidence and intuitive powers to cross the path.

The Empress

The third Major Arcana card depicts a queen sitting on a throne surrounded by nature's abundance in the form of rivers and streams and an enchanting verdant forest. The Queen on this card also symbolizes Mother Nature and/or the fertility goddess. Her robe, designed with pomegranate patterns, represents fertility (a pomegranate is full of seeds, so it stands for fertility). Aptly, the element governing the Empress card is earth.

The empress.
https://pixabay.com/es/illustrations/emperatriz-carta-de-tarot-s%c3%admbolo-6016923/

Venus rules the Empress, and therefore, it is the epitome of love and harmony. The figurine on the Empres's card has blonde hair with a crown of stars, a symbol of her connection to the magical, mystical realms. The Empress is a harbinger of blessings and abundance.

The keywords of an upright Empress card are nature, fertility, nurturing, motherhood, supportive, sensual, and/or committed romantic relationships. An upright Empress card indicates connecting with our femininity and sensuality to attract happiness and joy into our lives. The Empress is connected to Venus and, therefore, is associated with the Libra zodiac sign.

If you draw an upright Empress card, it means it is a time of self-care and self-compassion. It is also a card of pregnancy and motherhood. Of course, you must check out the cards in the entire spread to confirm this. Alternatively, it could indicate receiving or giving motherly, nurturing love. The Empress card also indicates new beginnings, including a new venture, idea, or project.

Reversed Empress card could indicate a loss of willpower, self-reliance, and inner strength because you have used up a lot of energy in caring for the welfare of others. A reverse card might mean that you need to stem the flow of excess nurturing and concern for others lest it goes overboard and you end up neglecting your own needs. Excessive concern for others could also result in smothering people you love with your care despite meaning well.

In Kabbalah, the Empress connects Binah and Chochmah, the path of the unity of the masculine and feminine. This is why the Empress is depicted as pregnant in some tarot decks. She unites the male and female to bring forth new life. Also, the Empress is the universal womb of creativity.

From the point of view of the Fool's journey, when he encounters the Empress, he recognizes the loving maternal figure, the one who nourishes and loves him unconditionally. He also learns about and feels grateful for Mother Nature, who showers her abundance on him. Like a baby who loves exploring new sensations and experiences, the Fool cannot stop exploring everything that enchants his senses.

The Emperor

The Emperor tarot card is depicted by a stoic ruler sitting on his throne, decorated with four rams' heads, the symbol of his zodiac sign, Aries. He carries a scepter in his left hand, symbolizing his right to rule. The orb that he carries in his right hand represents his kingdom. He is also depicted with a long, flowing beard representing his years of experience and the wisdom, knowledge, and authority he has gained to be the Emperor.

The emperor.
https://pixabay.com/es/illustrations/tarot-cartas-de-tarot-el-emperador-6129696/

The mountains behind him stand for his ambition and determination to greater leadership capabilities. These depictions are exactly opposite to the Empress card, which shows flowing rivers, nurturing care, and life-giving kindness and love. On the other hand, the Emperor rules with grit, determination, and sheer masculine force.

The keywords for the upright Emperor are structure, stability, protection, control, authority, and discipline. In reverse, the Emperor symbolizes tyranny, domineering control, stubbornness, and lack of focus and discipline. Drawing an upright Emperor card could indicate that, like him, you should be a strategic thinker for the problem at hand. You should create rules and regulations and think in a structured manner for optimal benefits.

Like the element fire that rules the Emperor, he is a reminder that you should guide but with a firm, authoritative hand lest things go out of control. It is also a reminder that although you might be in a position of power, like all kings and emperors, you are also here to serve the people you rule over. It is a call to act rationally and put your intellect over your mysterious instinctive powers. The Emperor in any of your tarot card sightings calls for you to break free from the shackles and limiting beliefs that bind you down.

Drawing an upright Emperor card indicates success in the future as you achieve your goals determinedly, methodically, and strategically. Suppose any of your cards depict the Emperor. In that case, it could indicate you'll soon be given a position of power, where methodical structure and order are needed for successful outcomes. You are to bring your years of wisdom and experience to the table to take it forward.

If you draw a reversed Emperor card, it could indicate the abuse of authoritative power. It could manifest in your life as an authoritative father, possessive partner (on the personal front), or an overly controlling boss (in the workplace). It could also mean that you are not as strong as a ruler and that you must take corrective action to that end.

In Kabbalah, the Emperor is the path between Chochmah and Tiferet. In this context, Chochmah is Wisdom (or the father figure), and Tiferet is the son. The father takes the manifesting energy from the Empress and passes it on to the individual, his son. The Emperor (masculine energy) and Empress (feminine energy) together bring about beauty and harmony in the world.

The Hierophant

The Hierophant card depicts a religious figure (could be the Pope or a leader of any religion) sitting in a formal religious environment like a temple or church. The initiating religious priest is shown wearing elaborate religious vestments. His right hand is depicted as being raised in blessing and benediction. He carries a cross with three horizontal lines representing the Trinity in his left hand. Two disciples or acolytes are seen sitting at his foot, learning from him.

The hierophant.
https://pixabay.com/es/illustrations/el-hierofante-tarot-tarjeta-magia-6016942/

The Hierophant, or the High Priest (ruled by Taurus and associated with Jupiter and Venus), is the male counterpart of the High Priestess. An upright Hierophant card keywords are conventionality, tradition, conformity, beliefs, knowledge, wisdom, and social groups. The keywords for reverse High Priest include unconventional, ignorance, new and untried methods, rebellion, and non-conformity.

Drawing an upright Hierophant card could indicate a desire to conform and follow set rules and regulations. It is an indication to stick to conventional methods and within orthodox boundaries. It is good to adapt to existing beliefs instead of trying innovation and newness.

Seeing a Hierophant in your tarot sightings could mean you'll be involved in religious ceremonies and rituals. This card clearly indicates well-established institutions and belief systems and tells you that you should stick to conformity and not break tradition for optimal outcomes.

Drawing a reversed Hierophant could indicate a feeling of being restricted or constrained by systems and structures. You might be experiencing a feeling of being trapped and that you have lost control of your life. You desire flexibility and want to break free from the shackles of tradition and convention. You feel tempted to break orthodoxy and turn rebellious. You feel the urge to defy social norms.

If you draw a reversed High Priest card, it mostly means you want to question well-established traditions and doctrines. In a love relationship, drawing a reversed Hierophant might indicate a stalemate in your relationship. On the professional front, it could mean having a stifling work atmosphere.

In Kabbalah, the Hierophant card is the path that connects Chochmah and Chesed. The main function of the High Priest is to connect the "As above, so below." He represents the Great Teacher of mysteries and secrets and unlocks the understanding between illusion and our sensory experiences.

The Lovers

The Lovers card is depicted with a male and female pair of humans who are being blessed and protected by an angel from above. The happy, loving couple is in the midst of a beautiful garden. The fruit tree with a snake hiding it standing behind the couple clearly indicates that it is the Garden of Eden, where the snake is trying its best to tempt the happy couple to fall into the trap of the pleasures of the flesh.

The lovers.
https://pixabay.com/es/illustrations/cartas-de-tarot-tarot-amantes-magia-6103697/

Gemini is the zodiac sign, Mercury is the planet of the Lovers card, and the air is the element. Air is the element of communication and mental activity, both of which are crucial for relationships and partnerships. The angel's blessings that fall between the couple appear to give a sense of balance to the lovers.

The keywords for upright Lovers are union/love/relationships and partnerships/ romance/and choices. The most important interpretation of the Lovers card is that the confidence, trust, unity, and love given to each other by the couple empowers them both, strengthening their relationship. The bond between a loving couple is strong and intimate.

Another important interpretation of the Lovers card is that of choice. It tells us we all must choose between opposites and mutually exclusive things. So, if you draw a Lovers card and love may not be the answer you seek for your question, then the indication could be that you are in a dilemma and have to consider all things carefully before making your choice.

The Lovers card is a step forward from the Hierophant card, which is all about rendering structure and order and following set rules and regulations. For the Fool, he has two new experiences with the Lovers card. For one, he experiences the power of sexual union with another person and learns the desire to create relationships. Until now, the Fool was more or less self-centered. But when he encounters the Lovers card, he feels the urge to reach out and become half of a loving couple.

Second, he has also to include decision-making in his life lessons. It teaches him that he needs to weigh all options before him, find out what values he stands for, and then make appropriate choices. He yearns to learn and grow by making his own choices.

In Kabbalah, the Lovers card is the path connecting Tifereth to Binah, signifying the connection between the heart (or the solar center of the self) to the great confluence of super consciousness. The Lovers card represents the union of the sun (masculine) and moon (feminine) energy.

Drawing a Lovers card could indicate that you found out what is important to you and made the correct choices. The Lovers card helps you develop your sense of purpose. A reverse Lovers card keywords include imbalance, disharmony, wrong choices, indecisiveness, conflicts, and detachments.

A reversed Lovers card could mean an internal or external conflict you are dealing with. Disharmony and imbalances might be making your life difficult. It indicates it is time for you to take a step back and take corrective measures before moving forward.

A reverse Lovers card could also indicate a breakdown in communication in your professional and personal relationships and partnerships. It could indicate that you are not taking responsibility for your actions and choices. You could be blaming others for your decisions instead of accepting the onus for the consequences of those decisions that are fructifying at this point in time.

The Chariot

The Chariot card is depicted by a charioteer seated inside his vehicle driven by two sphinxes, one black and one white. The warrior wears a crown on his head, a depiction of enlightenment. A crescent moon on his shoulders guides him on his way. The ambiance is that of a blue sky adorned with twinkling stars. The water element governs the card.

The chariot.
https://pixabay.com/es/illustrations/carruaje-tarot-tarjeta-magia-6016921/

A square emblazoned on the charioteer's chest keeps him stable and grounded. The black and white colors of the two sphinxes symbolize two opposing forces the rider has to control to bring about balance and stability to achieve his life purpose.

Keywords for the Chariot are determination, success, drive and ambition, self-control, discipline, and willpower. The Chariot card talks to you about overcoming challenges and obstacles to achieve your goals. It tells you that you can become victorious if you learn to control what is happening around you and that strength and determination are key elements in this journey.

If you draw a Chariot card, it indicates maintaining focus and discipline to achieve your dreams. The card indicates that the path to your destination will be full of twists and turns, and an ordered, structured approach is critical for success. The Chariot could indicate that you'll likely display stamina and confidence in your life. A hitherto hidden, aggressive aspect of your personality could find its way out to feed your confidence. While aggression is useful sometimes, it should also be reined in so you don't lose control over it.

Keywords for reversed Chariot are lack of direction and control, powerlessness, and forceful aggression. If you draw a reversed Chariot, it could mean you lack confidence and aggression in the current situation. The reverse card tells you that you are so caught up in your goals that you are not thinking things through in a structured manner. You are allowing your impulses to take control of your actions.

A reversed Chariot card could mean you do not have control over your life, and opposing forces are controlling you. It means you are taking things lying down because of which life is taking you where it pleases. It is a reminder you need to take charge of your chariot and drive it to the destination you want in the way you want.

In the Fool's journey, he has become an adult with a strong sense of identity by the time he reaches the Chariot card. He also has some mastery over himself and has developed the tools and skills needed for success and materialistic happiness. The Chariot represents the Fool's ego, his largest achievement so far. The charioteer is a proud man sitting confidently on his vehicle, riding victoriously toward his goals. He is the master of all that he surveys and appears to be in visible control of everything around him. He is filled with self-satisfaction and self-confidence for the moment, at least.

The Moon and the Cancer zodiac sign govern the Chariot. In Kabbalah, the Chariot is the path that connects Binah and Gevurah, the path through which the Spirit descends to manifest in the tangible world of human beings. In the reverse direction, the Chariot, after conquering the lower planes, is all set to cross the lower part of the Tree of Life and move into the higher planes of spiritual consciousness.

Strength

The Strength card is depicted by a woman who is fearlessly and confidently holding open the jaws of a ferocious lion. The woman dominates over the menacing lion, yet she is calm and confident, showing signs of total control of a given situation. She is courageous and yet shows love and compassion. The lion itself is a symbol of strength and courage, both of which are critical for the success of human beings. However, if these two elements are not reined in or checked in, then they could lead to destruction and chaos.

Strength.
https://pixabay.com/es/illustrations/tarot-cartas-de-tarot-fuerza-6129685/

The keywords of this card are confidence, bravery, inner power, and compassion. Drawing an upright Strength card means you have the courage and fortitude needed to get through the difficult times ahead. It indicates you have the calm and peace needed to overcome obstacles and challenges, becoming stronger and braver. It also shows you are very compassionate and kind, willing to take people along with you.

Patience is your forte as you wade through challenges to achieve your goals and dreams. Your fearlessness and resilience are your great strengths in your life path. Drawing an upright Strength card means that even though you might be going through a difficult time right now, your bravery and confidence will see you through. Success and stability will be your companions sooner than later.

The keywords for the reverse Strength card are lack of or low confidence, cowardice, self-doubt, aggression, and inadequacy. If you draw a reverse Strength card, it could indicate a time of fear and strife. You might find it difficult to harness your inner strength and power - and that fear and uncertainty may be ruling your life. A reversed Strength card could also mean that you are dealing with depression and sadness for some reason, because of which happiness and positive energy are being drained from your life.

The zodiac sign associated with the Strength card is Leo, and the element is fire. In the journey of the Fool, the Strength card plays a crucial role. He dips into its power time and again to deal with the challenges and obstacles he finds on his way. He begins to think that he may not be the master he thought he was.

His ego may have grown, but there is a lot more to learn and master in this world. His aggression and confidence sometimes take a beating, which is when he learns the value of patience, compassion, and kindness from the Strength card. He learns that willful and determined commanding attitudes must be balanced with tolerance and kindness for true happiness. The Fool learns to tame his ego.

In Kabbalah, the Strength card is associated with the path between Chesed and Gevurah. This path calls upon people to tame their animalistic instincts and embrace mercy and compassion to connect with their higher selves. It is the path that teaches you to lose your ego and get rid of arrogance and pride to move forward in life.

The Hermit

The Hermit card depicts an old man standing alone on a mountain peak with a lantern in his right hand and a staff in his left hand. The mountain represents his achievements and accomplishments. The peak represents his knowledge and the wisdom he has garnered through his experience. The lantern has a 6-pointed star inside it, the Star of Solomon, which stands for wisdom. Therefore, the Hermit is a symbol of spiritual achievement rather than materialistic success. The staff he holds represents the Hermit's authority and power.

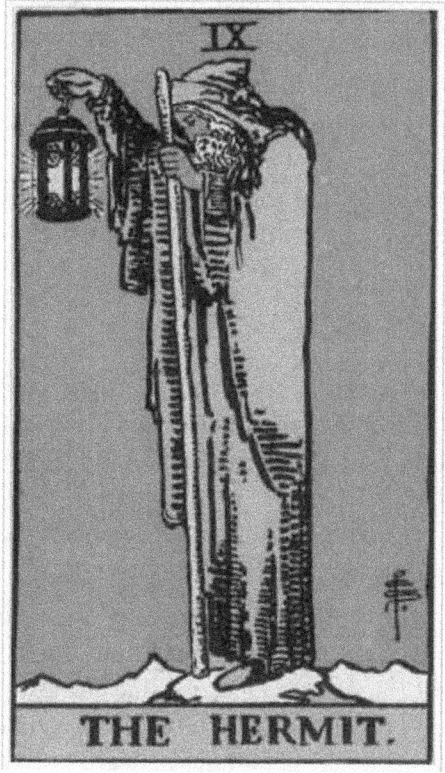

The hermit.
https://pixabay.com/es/illustrations/ermita%c3%b1o-tarot-tarjeta-magia-6016941/

The keywords for an upright Hermit card search for the authentic self, solitude, self-reflection, contemplation, and introspection. Seeing a Hermit card in your tarot sightings could indicate periods of solitude (not isolation or rejection). This time is for turning inward and seeking answers to your questions from within.

You must disconnect yourself from the crowds and the noise of your dreams and desires that threaten to throttle you. Step back from the noise and look within and seek answers. The Hermit card is a sign of walking alone through the darkness of your unconscious mind to find your true self.

If you draw a Hermit card, you desire solitude for contemplation and self-reflection. These moments of solitude help to clear the clutter of daily life so that you can reconnect with your true purpose and readjust your life path. It could also mean that a mentor or a coach could enter your life to help you.

A reversed Hermit card relates to loneliness, anti-social feelings, reclusiveness, isolation, and rejection. A reversed Hermit might mean you want to be left alone, which might be good. However, if not done correctly, being and feeling alone can lead to wrong outcomes for yourself and your loved ones.

Turning inward without proper support could lead to dangerous situations. People are known to have lost their sanity as they delved too deep into their psyche for their own good. The subconscious mind has dangers lurking to lure you into its abyss. Therefore, you must balance your inward search with support from fellow human beings.

From the point of view of your professional life, drawing a Hermit card could mean it is time to get to the bottom of something that has been bothering you for some time. Something needs to be done, and you have to get down to it before it takes on an uncontrollable element in your life.

In the Fool's journey, the Hermit card reminds us of the "Why" of human life. This card reminds him to find the true purpose of his life. Why is he here at all? He wants to know the answer not just to satiate his curiosity but with a deep desire to find his authentic self. With the Hermit card, the Fool turns inwards and digs deep into his emotions and thoughts, seeking answers. The sheen of the outside world is not attractive to him anymore, and he seeks something deeper and more meaningful. The Fool must undertake this journey alone.

The Hermit card is associated with Mercury, the zodiac sign Virgo, and the earth element. In Kabbalah, the Hermit card is the path from Tiferet to Chesed, the path of communication with the higher spiritual self. It is the path the lower self must undertake to find his authentic inner self.

The Wheel of Fortune

The Wheel of Fortune has a giant wheel in the center, which an eagle, angel, and bull surround, and a lion connected with four fixed signs, namely Aquarius, Scorpio, Leo, and Taurus. The four animals have wings which could indicate that they represent the four evangelists of Christianity.

Wheel of fortune.
https://pixabay.com/es/illustrations/tarot-cartas-de-tarot-6129686/

All four of the animals hold books in their hands which is symbolic of the Torah, the ultimate book of wisdom and knowledge. A lone sphinx rides on the giant wheel in the center. This is symbolic of cycles in your life. Sometimes, you are at the bottom, and sometimes at the top.

The Wheel of Fortune is associated with Saturn, the planet of structure and order, and the fire element. The upright Wheel of Fortune keywords are transformations, cycles, decisive periods, unexpected events or happenings, luck, and fortune. If you draw a Wheel of Fortune, it is a reminder that the cycles of life are not in your control. Everyone, from beggars to kings, is caught in these cycles, and none can avoid them. You must only learn to live in the moment and embrace everything happening in your life without resistance.

If you are in a good situation, then a bad one might come when the wheel turns, and the same thing is good when you are in a difficult situation. It reminds us that forces much larger than human forces are at work here, and we should give in to them. Regardless of where you land, the wheel will turn, and your position will change.

The keywords for a reversed Wheel of Fortune card are lack of control, bad luck, controlling or clinging to control, unpleasant delays, and changes. Drawing a reversed Wheel of Fortune indicates that good luck has not been in your life for a while now, and misfortunes have been following you. It reminds you that you are not in control and that you must simply wait for the wheel to turn again for better times.

It is important to remind yourself not to cling to control because bigger forces outside your purview of control are working here. Learn to let go and move on. The feeling of acceptance drives the wheel for another cycle with new positions for you and others.

From the point of view of the Fool's journey, he sees how things in this world are all interconnected. He has a vision of the world's design and how it moves on the Wheel of Fortune. He sees the intricate patterns and cycles that impact and affect us in different ways. He sees the universe in all its mysterious layers working together harmoniously. The Fool recognizes the importance of destiny and fate in his life and learns to embrace them wholeheartedly and without resistance.

In Kabbalah, the Wheel of Fortune card represents the path between Chesed (Mercy) and Netzach (Victory). The path connects the tangible personality to the higher, spiritual self through the pillar of mercy. The wheel symbolizes relentless cycles of birth, death, and rebirth.

The Justice Card

Astrologically speaking, the Justice card is associated with Libra, the zodiac sign of the balance and the air element. The Justice card speaks of law, truth, and fairness. The Lady of Justice sits on her judgment seat, holding scales in her left hand. The scales signify the importance of balancing logic with intuition to make accurate judgments.

Justice.
https://pixabay.com/es/illustrations/tarot-cartas-de-tarot-justicia-6129675/

The Lady of Justice stands for impartiality which is depicted by the double-edged sword she carries in her right hand. The square on her crown signifies clarity of thought, a key element during the dispensation of justice.

The upright Justice keywords are karma, accountability, consequences of actions, integrity, law, truth, and justice. If you draw the Justice card, it is a reminder that all your actions have consequences for yourself and others. There will always come a time in your life when your actions will be judged, and you'll either pay for them or get paid for them.

The meaning of drawing the Justice card depends on the situation and your feelings. For example, if you feel a sense of being wronged, then drawing the Justice card could bring you relief because it could indicate the time for the wrong to be righted. On the flip side, if you have wronged others, then drawing the Justice card could be a warning that your actions will be judged soon.

The reverse Justice keywords are retribution, revenge, lack of accountability, dishonesty, unfairness, corruption, and injustice. If you draw a Justice card in reverse, it could mean many things, including that you are living in denial or running from guilt. These feelings are rooted in past actions, and what you do today will bring about future consequences. You could take the reverse Justice card as an indication to make things right by others so that you have fair outcomes.

In the Fool's journey, the Justice card tells him to take a step back and look at the visions and lessons the Wheel of Fortune and Hermit cards taught him. What do these visions signify for him personally? He also looks back at his life, analyzes the cause and effects of his actions, and, most importantly, takes responsibility for himself. He has evolved as a man. He now knows the art of discernment, based on which he learns to make the right choices. The Fool learns to fight for equality in the form of the world's collective balance.

In Kabbalah, the Justice card is the path between Gevurah and Chesed, wherein Mercy tempers down severity through the hand of justice.

The Hanged Man

The Hanged Man is aware that his position is that of sacrifice. This sacrifice has to be made to move forward. It can be in the form of repenting for past mistakes. The sacrifice can be in the form of giving up certain things to become lighter than before, and moving forward becomes easy. Or it could be taking a step back, sacrificing some progress made earlier so that moving forward happens in a better way through recalculation and recalibration.

The hanged man.
https://pixabay.com/es/illustrations/hombre-ahorcado-tarot-tarjeta-magia-6016939/

The time lost in this act of taking a step back is not lost, but it is used to better understand his path so that the forward movement is significant and outcomes are more accurate than before. The Hanged Man is depicted as hanging upside down to symbolize the spiritual path that he is undertaking. Hanging upside down allows you to get a new perspective, something that people who are walking straight cannot see. This new perspective can lead to spiritual upliftment. The Hanged Man signifies this aspect of spirituality.

The Hanged Man also indicates a period of suspending action, especially during times of indecision. So, it is an indication to postpone certain actions until all aspects are understood well, and the actions can be implemented correctly. In fact, stalling action for a while is one of the best ways to ensure you get sufficient time to make critical decisions correctly.

The upright Hanged Man card keywords are uncertainty, lack of perspective and direction, waiting and contemplation period, martyrdom, and sacrifice. If you draw the Hanged Man card, it indicates a time of waiting and suspension. The card could be a suggestion to stall because it is the best thing to do at that point in time for the best results. It is a reminder that taking action is not always the best solution; sometimes, stalling works better.

The keywords for the reverse Hanged Man are avoiding or fear of sacrifice, apathy, disinterest, indifference, stalling, stagnation, and remaining still. If you draw a Hanged Man card in reverse, then it could indicate a time of indecision. It could also mean that you feel you have sacrificed a lot of time without any benefits. You might feel that you have given everything you have towards achieving something but to no avail.

The planet of the Hanged Man is Neptune, the element is water, and the zodiac sign is Pisces. From the perspective of the Fool's journey, the Hanged Man teaches him that life is not easily tamed, regardless of his daunting efforts to move forward in life. The Hanged Man teaches him that encountering losses and failures are imperative lessons of life that he must learn to succeed.

The Hanged Man card makes the Fool feel defeated for having sacrificed everything for nothing, or so it seems to him. That is when he realizes that relinquishing control over his life is the best way forward, and embracing humility, he inches slowly but surely towards wisdom. In Kabbalah, the Hanged Man represents the path between Gevurah and

Hod. It is the path of self-sacrifice that leads to resurrection and renewal.

The Death Card

The Death card is depicted by a skeleton wearing armor, riding a white horse, and holding up a black flag. The armor signifies that death is invincible and no one can defeat it. The horse he is riding on is white to signify purity. Death purifies all. The place beneath the death rider is strewn with corpses from all classes of society – from a beggar to a king – symbolizing that everyone becomes equal in the eyes of death.

The Death card is one of the most misunderstood tarot cards. It is feared without reason, and this is because most people take the Death card to signify death literally. In reality, this card could indicate one of the most positive times in your life. The Death card indicates the end of an old phase and the beginning of a new phase. It means it is time to close the door of one event in your life so you can open the door to another. It is time to put the past behind you and move toward future prospects.

Death.
https://pixabay.com/es/illustrations/cartas-de-tarot-tarot-muerte-magia-6103718/

The Death card could also indicate a change or transition in your life. An old version of "you" has to die to give birth to a new version of you.

It is not easy to do this, so feelings of fear are bound to arise. The uncertainty associated with changes can also bring fear. However, once you accept and embrace the changes, you'll see that all has happened for the better.

The keywords associated with the upright Death card are: endings/transformations and transitions/letting go/release. If you draw a Death card, it could indicate a time for transformation. It could indicate that you must be prepared to let go of old stuff, especially unhealthy attachments. The card tells you that holding on to decay and stagnation will only cause harm.

The reverse Death card is associated with fear of and resistance to change, negative patterns repeating in your life, decay, and stagnancy. If you draw a reverse Death card, it could indicate that you have been resisting changes. It could mean that you are scared of letting go of stuff and people. It is a reminder that clinging to things will limit your growth and development. A reverse Death card tells you to relook at your approach to your life or to a particularly nagging problem.

The Death card is associated with Scorpio, the element water, and the planet Pluto. In the Fool's journey, the Death card indicates loss and pain, which teaches him wisdom. He learns to let go of old, limiting habits and embrace new ones to improve his life. He learns to give up the frivolities and non-essential aspects of life. He learns to deal with endings and how to leave the remnants behind. He learns that "death" is a vital aspect of growth. He learns that everyone can rise from death towards newness and growth.

In Kabbalah, the Death card is the path between Tiferet and Netzach. It is the path wherein the lower energy of manifestation leads into the matter of the tangible world. Moving upward involves leaving behind the desire for Netzach (or Victory) and moving towards spiritual beauty.

The Temperance Card

A unisex angel with wings depicts the Temperance card. The unisex aspect signifies the merging or balancing of the opposites. The angel has one foot on earth (the physical world) and the other in water (the subconscious mind). The angel is also holding two cups which can be interpreted as her power to combine the waters of the conscious and subconscious minds into one infinite, seamless flow. This card is a representation of the union of dualities.

Temperance.
https://pixabay.com/es/illustrations/templanza-tarot-tarjeta-magia-6016917/

The keywords for an upright Temperance card are moderation, peace, balance, calm, harmony, middle path, and tranquility. Drawing an upright Temperance card means you have the wherewithal to remain calm even during stressful times. You are a master of tranquility and will not let any ruffle your feathers.

It indicates that you need a lot of patience to achieve your goals. It suggests balance and moderation for success. The Temperance card tells you to avoid all kinds of extremes and to remain balanced and calm. It indicates that you know what you want and how you want to achieve it. It also indicates that you are at peace with your life and everything happening there. Your ability to adapt is excellent, which empowers you to follow and achieve your dreams.

The keywords for a reverse Temperance card are excesses, imbalance, discord, haste, and recklessness. If you draw a reverse Temperance card, it could indicate some kind of imbalance in your life, resulting in anxiety and worry. When read with the other cards in the spread, you can even determine which aspects of your life are imbalanced. Drawing a reverse Temperance card could also be a warning that a certain path could lead to excesses and discord.

Another meaning of a reverse Temperance card is that you lack a long-term goal or vision in your life, which, in turn, gives no purpose to your life. Therefore, you could feel lopsided. It indicates that you need to step back and relook at your choices before moving forward.

The Temperance card is associated with Sagittarius, the fire element, and Jupiter. From the point of view of the Fool's journey, the Temperance card is a balancing point after swinging wildly since he discovered the Hermit card – until the loss and pain of the Death card. With the Temperance card, the Fool finds true peace and equilibrium, especially after experiencing the storms of the extremes. With the Temperance card, he has combined and balanced all aspects of his life and his personality to achieve wholesomeness. He feels secure and wise. In Kabbalah, the Temperance card is the path between Tiferet and Yesod.

The Devil

In the tarot deck, the Devil is depicted as half-goat, half-man with bat wings. An inverted pentagram is inscribed on his forehead. He appears to dominate and control a nude man and woman lying chained to a stone at his feet, signifying his control over human beings through sensual and materialistic pleasures. The flame on the man's tail and the bowl of grapes on the woman's tail signify their materialistic desires.

The devil.
https://commons.wikimedia.org/wiki/File:The_Illustrated_Key_to_the_Tarot_p._69.png

The man and woman have horns growing out of their head which signifies their connection to evil and devilish instincts as they spend a lot of time in the devil's company. However, despite having their materialistic desires satisfied by the devil, the man and woman are unhappy. Their nakedness is a matter of shame for them as their individual powers have been wrested from them by the devil.

The keywords for an upright Devil card are limitations, excesses, oppression, powerlessness, and dependency. If you draw a Devil card, it means you feel trapped. You are feeling empty and have no fulfillment in your life. It also could indicate that you are a slave to materialistic pleasures and desires. You don't know how to get rid of your excessive love for luxury and opulence eating into your true happiness.

The Devil card indicates that your materialistic greed is taking you into a bottomless rabbit hole, yet you don't know how to break free from the shackles. You seem to be losing control over your life. Substance addictions and abuse could also indicate such feelings of being trapped.

The keywords for a reversed Devil card are freedom, revelation, reclaiming control and power, and release. Drawing a reversed Devil card could indicate a time of self-awareness and a break from shackles. You might be tired of being trapped, and a little spark may have triggered the urge to break free.

While breaking free and releasing yourself from unwanted attachments is great, you must remember that it will not be easy. You must be prepared to make adjustments to break free and learn to be on your own instead of being dependent on things and people that might have given you some comfort even if they also gave you the feeling of being trapped. It is a time for self-assessment wherein you learn what works for you and what doesn't and how to handle what doesn't work for you.

In the Fool's journey, when he encounters the devil, he realizes he is encountering his own helplessness and ignorance. The Devil card reminds him that learning and growing is a relentless part of his journey, and sitting back on the assumption that he knows and has everything will prove fatal.

The Fool also learns that satisfying his material cravings is not enough for his happiness. His search for fulfillment continues, and he realizes that there is something far greater and more important than materialism and physical pleasures and joys. The Fool realizes how deeply bonded he is to materialism and that it is not easy to break free. His wisdom improves as he embraces the idea of overcoming the temptation to pursue his spiritual path. The Devil card is ruled by Saturn, the zodiac sign Capricorn. In Kabbalah, the Devil card is the path between Tiferet and Hod.

The Tower

The Tower card is depicted by a high tower located at the peak of a mountain. The tower has been struck by lightning and is on fire. Tongues of flame emanate from the windows, and people are desperate to escape from the tower. The tower's destruction is inevitable for a new, better tower to come up in its place.

You can compare the significance of these desperate jumping out of the inferno to the desperation of the two nude people chained to a stone at the foot of the Devil card. These people, too, want to escape life's trauma and turmoil. They want to escape the destruction caused by their greed and egoistic arrogance. The Tower card signifies that old ways must be cleared out to welcome something new.

The tower.
https://pixabay.com/es/illustrations/cartas-de-tarot-tarot-torre-magia-6103701/

The keywords for an upright Tower card are chaos, trauma, sudden changes, and disaster. Drawing an upright Tower card could indicate a momentous change and/or revelation in your life, which could turn your life upside down. However, it need not be something frightening or scary. The Tower card's core message could indicate a groundbreaking change for a much better life than before.

The Tower card sighting need not mean something terrible or painful. It is just a change, a sudden change, but something that is bound to end in a good way. The Tower card fills you with fear because it reminds you to give up some truths you had held dear until now, which is a scary prospect, at least in the beginning. Giving up old ways that you are used to and feel comfortable with takes time and effort, and that fills you with fear and uncertainty. The Tower card indicates that the old ways of your world are not useful to you anymore, and it is time to abandon them.

The keywords for a reversed Tower card are putting off the inevitable, resisting change, and avoiding disaster. If you draw a reversed Tower card, then it could indicate a big crisis looming ahead. More importantly, it indicates that you are struggling to come to terms with it. You don't like the prospect of encountering these changes. The Tower card warns you not to resist what is happening because the good things are at the end of transformations. It is a sign that you must let go of limiting beliefs that have held you back and find your inner strength to become a more authentic self than before.

From the point of view of the Fool's journey, he has realized he is in the Devil's grip. The Tower card is now telling him that only sudden changes can help him loosen himself from the tight clasp of the Devil. He has learned that the devil's fortress is now nothing more than a prison and that he must break down the walls to escape it. A severe shakeup is an essential element for this, the Fool realizes. The Tower's fire blasts ignorance, and he is reborn without the devil's shackles.

The Tower card is connected with Mars, the god of war, the fire element, and Aries and Scorpio. According to Kabbalah, the Tower card is the path between Netzach and Hod, from victory to individualism and intellect.

The Star

The Star card depicts a woman kneeling at the pond's edge, holding two containers. She is pouring water from the pond onto the dry land, which is lush and green, signifying the birth of new life, thanks to the woman's efforts at nurturing and caring.

One of the lady's feet is in the water, signifying her spirituality and mental and emotional strength. The other foot is on dry land representing her physical and practical abilities and strength. Behind the lady are seven small stars representing the seven chakras, or the energy centers in the human body.

The star.
https://pixabay.com/es/illustrations/cartas-de-tarot-tarot-estrella-6103699/

The keywords for an upright Star card are faith, hope, renewal, rejuvenation, and healing. If you draw an upright Star card, then it is an indication of hope and renewal. You'll realize that you are blessed abundantly. It is a reminder that you have everything needed within you to make things happen and to lead a fulfilling, happy life. The card reminds you to have faith because the universe is poised to fulfill your dreams and desires.

Also, if you draw an upright Star card, then it means you have passed a really big challenge. You have overcome this challenge without losing hope. The card tells you you are far more courageous and capable than you think. The card reminds you that you have discovered your resilience.

The keywords for a reversed Star card are negativity, despair, despondence, and lack of faith. If you draw a reversed Star card, you could feel that everything and everyone is working against you. The challenges you face seem insurmountable. You may have lost faith in yourself and the world around you. The reverse card is telling you not to lose faith. Instead, it asks you to dig deep within yourself and find hope to overcome the challenges.

In the Fool's journey, he is coming to terms with the falling Tower. As he picks up the pieces, he turns towards the goodwill he has earned until now and the blessings of the universe to heal and recover.

After the downfall of the Tower, the Fool is filled with serenity, and the Star card reflects this sense of peace he finds. The naked woman on the Star card signifies one whose soul is no longer hidden. The stars above are like a beacon of hope. This fills the Fool with enough trust to counter and replace all the negative energies of the Devil card. His faith is restored, both in himself and the world.

In Kabbalah, the Star card represents the path between Netzach and Yesod, from victory to intuition and dreams. The Star card is associated with Aquarius, the air element, and the planet Uranus.

The Moon

The Moon card depicts a path that leads one to the far horizon. The path is flanked by a dog on one side (representing our tamed, civilized, domesticated nature) and a wolf on the other side (representing our wild, untamed nature). Crawfish emerge from the pond in the card. Two towers on the horizon signify the dualities of life. Interestingly, the similarities of the towers symbolize the difficulty we have in discerning between good and evil. The path that leads into the far horizon is a fine line that separates the conscious and unconscious.

The moon.
https://pixabay.com/es/illustrations/cartas-de-tarot-tarot-luna-magia-6103698/

The keywords for an upright Moon card are intuition, illusion, uncertainty, secretive, complexities, and the unconscious mind. The Moon card represents the dark, which could be interpreted as you walk on the path, unsure of where it is leading you. There could be dangers lurking in the vicinity. The crawfish represents you. The moonlight brings you clarity and understanding. You must allow your intuition to guide you through the dark path.

Drawing a Moon card is a sign of becoming aware of the situation and surroundings and handling the fears and uncertainties in your mind. The card is a warning not to let your inner turmoil lead you to wrong decisions and choices. It reminds you to let go of deep memories and fears hidden in your subconscious mind.

Another interesting indication if you draw an upright Moon card is the existence of an illusion, some kind of hidden truth that needs to be unraveled before it gets the better of you. Alternatively, it could indicate that what you see is an illusion and all is not as it seems.

The keywords for a reversed Moon card are deception, fear, misunderstanding, anxiety, and clarity. If you draw a reversed Moon card, it could indicate that some dark aspects (like the darker side of the Moon) are present in your life. These dark aspects could be in the form of turmoil, confusion, or sadness. Your uncertainty in dealing with them enhances their effects on your life.

A reversed Moon card is a warning that you must deal with your fears and anxieties and that you could misinterpret messages and/or signals. Another interpretation when you draw a reversed Moon card is that all the negative energies are fading away, and you can see the light at the end of the tunnel.

In the journey of the Fool, the Moon card represents vulnerability. Until the previous card, the Fool had learned well from the lessons that life taught him, and now he was calm and serene. This sense of calm itself causes his vulnerability and makes his vision illusionary under the light of the Moon. The Moon card makes the Fool dreamy, making him susceptible to fantasy and distortion of the truth.

The Moon card is associated with the Moon, the zodiac sign Aquarius, and the water element. In Kabbalah, the Moon card is the path between Netzach and Malchut, between love, connection, victory, and the physical, materialistic world.

The Sun

The Sun card depicts dawn, the rays of hope and sunlight that follow the night's darkest hour. It represents fulfillment and optimism. When you see the sunrise, you feel a sense of hope filling your body and mind. The Sun card signifies the same feelings. A naked child playing joyfully represents the innocence that comes when we are aligned with our authentic selves when we have nothing to hide. The child is riding a white horse, which signifies purity, nobility, and strength.

The sun.
https://pixabay.com/es/illustrations/cartas-de-tarot-tarot-sol-magia-6103700/

The keywords for the upright Sun card are vitality, confidence, success, truth, happiness, celebration, and optimism. You will likely get abundance and success if you draw an upright Sun card. The card renders vitality and happiness to you. You can expect joy and happiness to come into your life.

It also indicates you are feeling fulfilled, which, in turn, makes you inspire others to work towards their fulfillment. Your joy attracts people to you, and you happily spread your energy to one and all. You radiate love to everyone who comes in contact with you. If you draw a Sun card, it indicates that you are feeling highly confident in yourself and your achievements. Life is good as the sun's radiating light shines upon you.

The keywords for a reversed Sun card are over-enthusiasm, unrealistic expectations, pessimism, negativity, pride, and blocked happiness. If you draw a reversed Sun card, then it could mean a time of sadness. It need not necessarily stem from sad events but from the fact that you find it difficult to see the happiness in your life. You are prevented from feeling confident of your achievements, even if your goals are substantial. Certain setbacks could impact your confidence.

A reversed Sun card could also indicate that you have unrealistic expectations; therefore, fulfillment and happiness evade you. Having an overly optimistic view of things could result in disappointment, and a reversed Sun card indicates that. It is a reminder for you to be realistic about things.

The Sun card is associated with the Sun, the fire element, and the zodiac sign, Leo. In the Fool's journey, this card represents that part of his journey cloaked in happy experiences and wisdom. He learned the importance of living and enjoying every moment of his life, and he is grateful to the cosmos for everything.

He realizes that the power and light of the Sun dispel darkness from every nook and corner of his being. Confusions are cleared, and he feels enlightened. He is enthusiastic and filled with vitality and vibrant energy. He is riding on a white horse, eagerly looking forward to a new day and the experiences it will bring.

In Kabbalah, the Sun card connects Hod with Yesod and Splendor with Foundation. This path is an activating force of one's personality as you feel splendorous and yet feel grounded and stable. It is the path of the intellect.

The Judgment Card

The Judgment card depicts Judgment Day as described in various religions. The card shows men, women, and children awaiting their judgment as they rise from their graves in answer to Gabriel's call. Their hands are outstretched, indicating the people are ready to take whatever judgment is given to them. This card reflects the fact that the consequences of your actions cannot be escaped. Judgment will come one day or another.

Judgment.
https://pixabay.com/es/illustrations/tarot-cartas-de-tarot-juicio-6129676/

The upright Judgment card keywords are reckoning, purpose, reflection, self-evaluation, and awakening. If you draw an upright Judgment card, it indicates a time of self-reflection and self-evaluation, both of which are essential to better understand what is happening in your life and your responses and reactions to them.

It indicates that only when you understand your *now*, can you move more confidently into your future, choosing the right path. With self-reflection comes understanding, and with understanding comes the need to make changes and adjustments so that your life path is reset accurately to where you want it to go. These changes and adjustments could be small ones that affect only you or big ones that impact your loved ones too.

When you draw an upright Judgment card, it is a reminder that all are bound to face difficult choices that could have lasting impacts on their lives and those of their loved ones. It reminds you that actions have set your life on an entirely new and unexpected path, and this is the time to face this truth. The card tells you it is time to let go of the past and move on with renewed hope and confidence because every end is a new beginning.

The reversed Judgment card keywords are low self-awareness, self-doubt, and self-loathing. If you draw a reversed Judgment card, it could mean you judge yourself harshly, creating a hazy vision for yourself. For some reason, you hate yourself. In such situations, you are so caught up judging yourself that you miss out on opportunities that have been as clear as day to everyone else but you. It indicates that you are likely to have a period of slow momentum.

Another meaning of drawing a reversed Judgment card is that you must take time out for self-reflection. You must take time out to see how your life is turning out and evaluate the events and happenings. It is time to ask yourself if you are learning life lessons well. The reverse card could be telling you that you have been judging yourself too harshly for your own good. It tells you to forgive yourself for your past actions, let them go, and move on.

The Judgment is ruled by Pluto, the god of the underworld, the fire element, and the zodiac sign Scorpio. In the Fool's journey, he has almost reached the end. This card indicates that he must stop and test his own integrity. The card gives him moral and ethical takeaways from his entire journey.

Here, the Fool is reborn after shedding his false ego and arrogance. His true self is revealed to him, and he realizes that not fear but joy is the core of human life. He forgives himself and feels absolved, knowing and accepting that his core self is pure and sinless. The Judgment card reminds him that his day of reckoning has come, and he needs to embrace the judgments and move into a new future.

In Kabbalah, the Judgment card is the path between Hod and Malchut, between individualism, intellect, and the material, physical world. It is the path that connects your individualism with the physical external world so that you can find an identity for yourself.

The World Card

The World card is depicted with a figure dancing in the center, holding a wand in each hand and one leg crossed over the other. The female figure symbolizes balance and evolution. She also represents fulfillment and completion. However, these two are not static forms but dynamic ones that keep changing and evolving eternally.

The world.
https://pixabay.com/es/illustrations/cartas-de-tarot-tarot-mundo-magia-6103702/

The green wreath around the lady represents success, while the red ribbon around the wreath signifies infinity and eternity. The four figures at the four corners of the World card represent four zodiac signs, namely Taurus, Leo, Scorpio, and Aquarius. They also represent the four evangelicals and the four elements. Therefore, the World card represents the harmonious balance between all the energies of the world.

The keywords for the upright World card are a sense of belonging, fulfillment, completion, and wholesomeness. You can expect fulfillment and completion if you draw an upright World card from your tarot deck. It symbolizes a time when your outer and inner worlds are in sync with each other, and you feel whole and complete.

The card tells you that all your efforts are being fructified and your rewards are starting to come in. It also indicates the completion of a major milestone in your life. It tells you you should be proud of achieving this milestone because you had to overcome many challenges.

An upright World card could indicate that you have successfully completed a long-term project or life event. It could mean marriage, the birth of a child, completing your graduation, or even a big project at the workplace. The World card also indicates that you want to give back to society in some way or another. You are committed to making this world a better place.

The keywords for the reversed World card are a sense of incompletion, lack of closure and achievement, and a sense of emptiness. A reversed World card indicates that you are at the end of some achievement but filled with a sense of emptiness. You feel that all the pieces are not coming together as you envisaged them. You feel some pieces are missing or are in the wrong place. Something is preventing you from feeling accomplished.

The World card is governed by Saturn, the earth element, and three zodiac signs, including Taurus, Capricorn, and Virgo. In Kabbalah, the World card is the path between Yesod and Malchut, between dreams and intuition and the material, physical world. It connects your dreams to practicality.

In this last card of his journey, the Fool learns to take a step back, evaluate, feel the sense of accomplishment of completing the journey, and then prepare himself for the next venture or adventure. He knows that his cycle is complete, the future is full of promise, and he is ready to take the plunge again.

Therefore, the Fool's journey was fulfilling, and his perseverance and hard work paid off. He is not a naive person anymore. He has learned wisdom, picked up knowledge and important life lessons, and has evolved a lot since the start of his journey.

Chapter 7: Meet the Cards II: Four Suites

The 22 Major Arcana cards deal with the larger aspects of your life, while the 56 Minor Arcana cards guide you through your daily, routine trials and tribulations of life. Do not be mistaken by the word "minor" because the impacts of these cards are anything but that.

The cards in the Minor Arcana offer significant insights into your present situation and how you can change or improve your actions for better outcomes. The energies of the Minor Arcana cards in your life are temporary. These energy dynamics change or move depending on your actions and their immediate consequences.

The Minor Arcana is divided into four suites, namely:

- The Suit of Cups

The Suit of Pentacles The Suit of Swords The Suit of Wands Each of the four suits has the following cards:

- Number cards from 1 (or Ace) to 10
- Court cards consisting of the Page, Knight, Queen, and King

The Suit of Cups

The Suit of Cups represents your intuition, emotions, and creativity. In Jungian terms, the Suit of Cups refers to our emotional responses and reactions to stimuli. This suit deals with your relationships and partnerships. It gives you insights into your emotions, emotional dealings, and interactions with others. The Suit of Cups is associated with the water element, fluid and agile.

Ace of Cups - The keywords for Ace (or One) of Cups are new beginnings, fertility and pregnancy, and celebrations. If you draw an upright Ace of Cups, it indicates new beginnings in romantic relationships and partnerships. It indicates a time of joy, empathy, and compassion. Good news could be on the way to you.

If you draw a reversed Ace of Cups, it could be a harbinger of sadness. It also indicates repressed emotions and pain of some kind. You could receive sad, upsetting news. Relationships may not be in the best state of your life. In Kabbalah, Aces or Number one is associated with Keter, the Crown.

Two of Cups - This card is very positive, and if you draw it, it means your life is joyous and happy. Keywords for an upright Two of Cups are mutual attraction and unified romantic relationships and friendships. It also signifies unity in romantic relationships, respect, and affection in partnerships and friendships. If you see Two of Cups in a spread, it could indicate harmony and balance. Reversed Two indicates disharmony, imbalance, argument, and breakups. Number Two is associated with Chochmah or wisdom.

Three of Cups - An upright Three of Cups signifies collaborations, friendship, and celebrations. In the reverse, it signifies independence and "me-time." If you draw an upright Three of Cups, it could mean that someone from your past life is coming back into your life. It signifies groups of people coming together, such as at parties and celebrations. Celebrations and parties could get canceled if you draw a reversed Three of Cups.

Four of Cups - An upright Four of Cups signifies contemplation, meditation, and revaluation. In the reverse, the keywords are withdrawal, introspection, and retreating. Suppose you draw an upright Four of Cups. In that case, it could indicate missed opportunities leading to regret and contemplation on what went wrong. When you see this card in your spread, it is a message for you not to miss out on the opportunities and to grab them. In reverse, the Four of Cups could mean a reversal of bad things. You may have felt stuck in a rut, and this card indicates the difficult time is coming to an end. Four is associated with Chesed, or Mercy, in Kabbalah.

Five of Cups - An upright Five of Cups' keywords are pessimism, failure, regret, and disappointment. A reversed Five of Cups' keywords are self-forgiveness, moving on, and personal setbacks. The Five of Cups indicates a lot of negative emotions, whether you see an upright or reversed card. When you draw a Five of Cups, it means you are focusing on the negative aspects of your life a lot more than needed. An unwelcome sadness is impending in your life. Or you could feel isolated and lonely.

If you draw a reverse Five of Cups, the card tells you it is time to forgive yourself, learn your lessons, and move on. There is no use moping about the past. If you are really struggling with depression, then it might make sense to use the services of a professional therapist. Five is associated with Gevurah or severity, which is aligned with sadness and disappointment.

Six of Cups - An upright Six of Cups signifies childhood memories, visiting the past, and innocent joyfulness. It represents nostalgia. If you draw an upright Six of Cups, it could mean that your past influences you. A reversed Six of Cups signifies living in the past, being overly serious, and forgiveness. Drawing a reversed Six of Cups could mean you are ready to move on, leave home, or start fresh. Six, in the Tree of Life, stands for Tiferet or beauty.

Seven of Cups - An upright Seven of Cups represents choices, opportunities, illusions, and wishful thinking. Drawing an upright Seven of Cups means you have multiple possibilities ahead of you. But it could also mean you are living in a fantasy and indulging in wishful thinking. A reversed card could indicate being overwhelmed by many choices and alignment with your personal choices. A reversed drawing could also mean that you are getting clarity after living in a world of wishful thinking for a while. Number seven is associated with Netzach.

Eight of Cups - An upright Eight of Cups could be abandonment, escapism, withdrawal, and disappointment. A reversed Eight of Cups could mean aimlessly drifting along, indecisiveness, walking away from people and situations, and the desire to try one more time before giving up. Number Eight is associated with Hod.

Nine of Cups - Nine of Cups signifies satisfaction, contentment, and gratitude. If you pick an upright Nine of Cups, your wishes and dreams will likely come true. A reversed Nine of Cups means you find inner happiness and materialistic pleasures. It could also indicate indulgence and dissatisfaction. A reversed Nine of Cups is usually seen as a bad omen where there are fears that your dreams will come crashing down. Number Nine is associated with Yesod.

Ten of Cups - An upright Ten of Cups keywords' are harmony, alignment, blissful relationships, and divine love. A reversed Ten of Cups indicates misaligned values and principles, disconnection with people, and struggling relationships. In general, a Ten of Cups translates to true happiness and fulfillment. A reversed Ten of Cups is not a great sign and could mean that conflicts and arguments will replace happiness and contentment. Number Ten is associated with Malchut.

The Suit of Pentacles

The Suit of Pentacles deals with finances, wealth, and profession. It gives you insights into your financial wealth and career details. It also deals with your external surroundings and how you deal with and respond to them. For example, the cards drawn from this suit will tell you how you deal with money, health, and career-related issues.

How do you see your job? Is it just a way of earning money, or do you treat it as a service? The Suit of Pentacles cards answers these questions. The Suit of Pentacles, at a deeper level, deals with your self-esteem and ego. It is associated with the earth element.

At a Jungian level, the Suit of Pentacles is associated with your sensory information and experiences. How do you react to the information and stimuli your five senses feel or get? It is an indication of your pleasure and materialistic needs and desires and how you go about achieving them. The negative aspects of this suit involve being overly materialistic, greedy, and clingy.

Ace of Pentacles - In general, an upright Ace of Pentacles indicates prosperity and new beginnings. If you draw an upright Ace of Pentacles, it means any new venture you begin is likely to be successful, or a new venture is in the offing. The keywords of an upright Ace of Pentacles are a new career or financial opportunity and abundance.

In reverse, the Ace of Pentacles indicates a lack of vision, planning, foresight, and lost opportunities. If you draw a reverse Ace of Pentacles, it could mean you are not doing enough to prevent prospects from falling through the cracks. You lack focus and control. It is a warning to get your act together.

Two of Pentacles - In the upright position, the Two of Pentacles refers to adaptability and prioritization. It means you are trying to balance the ups and downs in your life and have the adaptability and organizing abilities to do so. It also means there is a struggle between your priorities and those of other people in your life, maybe a loved one or a good friend.

In reverse, it indicates disorganization and a need for reprioritization. Drawing a reverse Two of Pentacles could mean you are biting off more than you can chew. It is a warning for you to go back to the drawing board and reprioritize your stuff. Also, it means you need to save or put aside resources for a rainy day.

Three of Pentacles - An upright Three of Pentacles translates to teamwork, collaboration, learning, and apprenticeship. It means you are working hard to learn and collaborate with other people in your life to achieve success on a solid foundation of knowledge. In the reverse, it stands for working in isolation and misalignment. It indicates that you are not learning from your mistakes because you feel overwhelmed.

Four of Pentacles - An upright Four of Pentacles stands for conservatism and traditionalism, saving money for future security, scarcity, and control. It indicates that you are holding on to situations, people, and possessions. You have a problem with letting go and a desire to control yourself in unhealthy, toxic ways.

In the reverse, it means self-aggrandizement through overspending and greed. It could mean you are engaging in reckless behavior leading to potential harm. However, it also means you have stopped trying to control things and have let go.

Five of Pentacles - An upright Five of Pentacles indicates poverty, financial losses, and worry. It indicates a time of hardship and negativity in your life through job loss and unemployment. In the reverse, it stands for restoring faith and spirituality in your life and recovering financial losses. It stands for a time of recovery from your financial struggles. It also means you are willing to let go of toxic people.

Six of Pentacles - An upright Six of Pentacles indicates a sense of sharing, generosity, and charity. If you draw a Six of Pentacles, it could mean you'll receive generous gifts. Also, you feel like sharing your resources generously. In the reverse, it stands for unpaid debts, only giving and not getting anything back, and self-care. It could mean that someone is giving you gifts but with conditions that may or may not harm you.

Seven of Pentacles - In an upright position, the Seven of Pentacles stands for sustainable results and a long-term view. Drawing an upright Seven of Pentacles means that your hard work and perseverance are beginning to pay off. In reverse, it signifies limited success and the lack of a long-term view. It indicates that your hard work is getting you very little reward or success. It could mean that you are not finishing what you started.

Eight of Pentacles - An upright Eight of Pentacles translates to repetitive work, apprenticeship, and skill-building. It indicates a period of hard work and diligent commitment. You are picking up skills that will be of immense use in the future. In the reverse, it signifies laziness and lack of effort. It also indicates misdirected activity. It could also indicate that you are so focused on one area of your life that you are completely neglecting other equally important aspects.

Nine of Pentacles - In an upright position, the Nine of Pentacles stands for self-sufficiency and financial independence. It indicates freedom and stability. You have worked hard and diligently to achieve success. In the reverse, it stands for being overly invested in your work or profession. You lack confidence and stability. It could also mean that you are getting rewards for which you have not worked hard, and these rewards may not last.

Ten of Pentacles - An upright Ten of Pentacles signifies wealth and financial success and family aspects. You find success and happiness in all aspects of your life, especially in the materialistic areas. You feel closely connected with your family. In the reverse, it represents financial losses and wealth and power's dark side. There is instability and insecurity in your life. A reversed Ten of Pentacles is a warning to avoid shady financial and power deals.

The Suit of Swords

The Suit of Swords deals with your actions, thoughts, verbal expressions, and communication in general. It deals with the mental aspects of human life, including the mind and intellect. The cards drawn from this suit give you insights into asserting your power, expressing yourself, communicating your ideas, and making decisions.

Swords are usually double-edged, and the Suit of Swords symbolizes the fine balance you need to maintain between power and intellect for success and happiness. In Jungian terms, the Suit of Swords deals with your cognitive function and how you process information and data in your mind.

Ace of Swords - An upright Ace of Swords signifies new ideas, breakthroughs, and success. Drawing an Ace of Swords indicates you have great mental clarity and focus, allowing you to make correct decisions. In the reverse, it stands for clouded judgment and doubting ideas and thoughts. Drawing a reversed Ace of Swords means you are confused and led by misinformation.

Two of Swords - An upright Two of Swords indicates an impasse. It signifies that you are weighing options and difficult decisions. It also means you are avoiding making difficult decisions. You are at a crossroads, sitting on the fence, unable to decide. In the reverse, the Two of Swords stands for confusion and indecision. There are delays and postponements. Overwhelming fear and worry are preventing you from making the right decision.

Three of Swords - An upright Three of Swords signifies sorrow, heartbreak, grief, and emotional pain. If this card appears in your spread, a period of difficulty and hardship is indicated. In the reverse, it signifies forgiveness, the release of sorrow, and optimism. A reverse Three of Swords represents overcoming sorrow and heartaches.

Four of Swords - An upright Four of Swords indicates rest, relaxation, and recuperation through meditation and contemplation. Drawing this card upright means a period of stress and anxiety that can be overcome through meditative rest and relaxation. This card tells you that your difficulties are not as bad as you think. You just need to relax, and solutions will emerge. In the reverse, it signifies a period of reawakening and rejuvenation. After some solitude and isolation, you are ready to rejoin the world.

Five of Swords - An upright Five of Swords indicates a desire to win at all costs, competitiveness, conflicts, and disagreements. This card is not really a good sign because it indicates defeat and surrender, but more importantly, a self-sabotaging attitude. It also means there is a lot of stress and conflict in your life. In the reverse, it is a good omen because it indicates reconciliation and making amends. It tells you that the time to end conflicts is near.

Six of Swords - An upright Six of Swords represents a rite of passage, the release of burdens, baggage, and transition. If you draw an upright

Six of Swords, it means you'll overcome grief and challenges. You can expect your problems to settle down. You'll be relieved of your burdens. It could indicate travel or a journey, even if it is to escape from troubles for a while. In the reverse, it signifies resistance to change and unfinished tasks. It indicates troubling times ahead and a lack of progress. It could also indicate disruptions and interruptions in travel.

Seven of Swords - The keywords for an upright Seven of Swords are deception and betrayal. If you draw this card upright, it generally means you'll encounter trickery and cheating. It signifies mental manipulations and scheming attitudes. It indicates getting away with some wrongdoing. In the reverse, the keywords are turning over a new leaf and becoming conscientious. It means you regret certain past actions and want to make amends.

Eight of Swords - An upright Eight of Swords translates to self-restrictions, negative self-talk, and a sense of being victimized. If you draw this card, it could mean you feel trapped and pushed into a corner. You feel persecuted and cornered. In the reverse, it indicates freedom from persecution and finding solutions to break free from the sense of entrapment.

Nine of Swords - An upright Nine of Swords translates to anxiety, fears, and worries. The card tells you that your fears may not be well-grounded and based on real problems. It just indicates your inner fears, more likely to be baseless than not. It represents stress and negative thinking. In the reverse, it signifies light at the end of a dark tunnel. It is an indication that your stress and fears are ending. You'll learn to cope well.

Ten of Swords - An upright Ten of Swords signifies hurtful endings, loss, and betrayal. It represents ruin and failure. It could indicate that someone in your life is playing a needless martyr filling you with guilt and depression. In the reverse, Ten of Swords stands for things improving, your mindset clearing and getting better, and surviving the worst.

The Suit of Wands

The Suit of Wands depicts your passions and energy levels. Cards from this suit give you insights into your spirituality and life purpose. They also indicate new and innovative ideas. In Jungian terms, the Suit of Wands deals with our intuition and instincts, the mysteries and secrets of our subconscious, and spiritual aspects and abilities. The Suit of Wands is associated with fire, the hot and unpredictable element. In the same way, this suit deals with our passions and creativity, and if not used well, it can destroy, and if used well can create useful, productive stuff for us.

Ace of Wands - An upright Ace of Wands signifies new beginnings and growth potential. It indicates a time for action driven by passion and enthusiasm. It means you feel bold and passionate about trying new stuff. In the reverse, it stands for setbacks and delays. It could herald disappointing and sad news as well.

Two of Wands - An upright Two of Wands stands for progress, decision-making, and future planning. If you draw an upright Two of Wands, it could indicate having to choose between two paths. It could also indicate overseas travel and sudden journeys. In reverse, it stands for lack of planning and fear of change and the unknown. It also means you have restricted options, and travels could get canceled or delayed.

Three of Wands - An upright Three of Wands indicates overseas travel, expansion, and foresight. It signifies adventure, freedom, and travel, especially to foreign lands and romantic holidays. It is a card of self-belief and self-confidence. In the reverse, it means moving back home or returning from travel. It also warns you about a lack of foresight or planning for the future.

Four of Wands - An upright Four of Wands signifies homecoming, celebration, and joy. It signals parties, weddings, and celebratory events. It indicates a time of stability and security and a time for families and communities to come together. In the reverse, it stands for postponement and/or delays in celebratory events, jilted romances, and leaving home. A reverse Four of Wands could indicate self-doubt and low self-esteem.

Five of Wands - An upright Five of Wands indicates disagreement, conflicts, competition, and tensions. It indicates struggles, opposition, aggression, and flaring tempers. You can expect a lack of cooperation and petty arguments. In the reverse, it stands for ending conflicts and arguments and finding common ground for solutions.

Six of Wands - An upright Six of Wands indicates self-confidence, public recognition, and success. It is an advantageous period for you, and you could win awards and accolades. You could obtain a leadership position in your life. In the reverse, Six of Wands represents failures and losses. You may lose out on awards and recognitions.

Seven of Wands - An upright Seven of Wands' keywords are challenge, protection, and perseverance. Drawing this card means you'll stand your ground and fight for what you believe. It also indicates that someone is harassing and attacking you. In the reverse, the Seven of Wands indicates surrendering your beliefs. It means you are exhausted and worn out. It could indicate a time when you have lost control and power.

Eight of Wands - An upright Eight of Wands indicates fast-paced transitions, movements, and even air travel. It signifies hastiness and rush. It is a card of fast-paced movements, being energetic, and getting carried away. In the reverse, this card stands for slow progress and low energy.

Nine of Wands - An upright Nine of Wands stands for courage, resilience, and a test of faith. If you draw this card, it means you are halfway through your goal, and your energy is totally drained. You want to give up, but this card reminds you of your courage and resilience. It tells you that your faith is being tested and not to give up. In the reverse, Nine of Wands stands for stubbornness and rigidity. It warns of an uncompromising attitude that can only lead to more harm than good.

Ten of Wands - An upright Ten of Wands indicates extra responsibilities and burdens. Something that was good initially has now become a huge burden leading to stress and anxiety. However, the card also tells you that the end is in sight, and soon you'll be relieved of your burdens. In the reverse, Ten of Wands stands for excessive responsibility and carrying a cross that is too heavy to bear. It could also indicate that it is time to let go and free yourself of your burdens.

Now that you are familiar with the Four Suites and their number cards, it is time to move on to the Court cards discussed in the next chapter.

Chapter 8: Meet the Cards III: Court Cards

The court cards consist of the King, Queen, Knight, and Page; although they belong to the Minor Arcana, too, they set themselves apart from the other cards of each suit.

Understanding the Court Cards

The four court cards appear in each of the four suits. The four represent different figures in a royal court, and a tarot reading can symbolize different people impacting your life in different ways.

The King is the traditional monarch and represents control and authority. The King takes charge of a group and uses his various leadership skills, such as diplomacy, courage, sensitivity, magnanimity, power, maturity, and logic, to lead a team.

The Queen is the court's caregiver and nurturer. The drawing of a Queen card could indicate that either you need the love and care that she can give or that someone in your life is offering loving, protective care to you.

The Knight is the young warrior of a royal court who is known to act rashly and violently but often decisively and for the sake of honor. If you draw Knight Cards, then fast-paced action of some kind could be indicated in your life.

The Page is the youngest member and belongs to the lowest hierarchy in the royal court. He is known for his innocence and one with the most potential for growth and development. Drawing a Page card could be an indication of incoming news or messages. Alternatively, it could be a self-revelation. Further, this card represents any young person or child in your life.

In Kabbalah, the King is the father figure associated with Chochmah, who unites with the Queen, the mother figure associated with Binah. The two of them united to produce the Page (in Kabbalah, the Page is the princess) and the Prince (the Knight card). The Knight is associated with Tiferet, and the Page with Malchut.

The Court Cards of Cups

The King of Cups represents diplomacy and sensitivity. This card in the upright position represents kindness and compassion. Drawing this card means finding the right balance between your heart and intellect. In the reverse, the King of Cups indicates an emotionally immature state of mind with a lack of emotional maturity.

The Queen of Cups signifies empathy and love. Drawing an upright Queen of Cups could indicate a woman who will support and care for you. It is also a card that warns you to be mindful of how you treat yourself and others. In reverse, the Queen of Cups stands for lack of trust and feelings of insecurity.

The Knight of Cups stands for honor and romance. This card carries a lot of excitement through invitations to proposals, events, and other big offers. In the reverse, it signifies heartbreak, unrequited love, and deception. If you draw a reverse Knight of Cups, you could have a one-night stand.

The Page of Cups represents innocence and infatuation. The Page of Cups is a messenger bringing happy news and messages in the form of invitations and potentially useful information. In the reverse, this card stands for bad news and broken dreams.

The Court Cards of Wands

The King of Wands signifies leadership and courage. Drawing a King of Wands indicates that you'll have the energy and enthusiasm to accomplish what you have set out to do. You lead the way for others to follow. In the reverse, it represents boorish and bullying behavior. You are setting a bad example for others.

The Queen of Wands stands for creativity and sensuality. Drawing this card could mean you are getting a lot of work done, thanks to your high energy and optimistic nature. You are always on the go. In the reverse, it stands for pessimism and a temperamental attitude. You have taken on more than you can manage and are exhausted.

The Knight of Wands signifies impulsive adventure. If you draw the Knight of Wands, you feel fearless and raring to go. It is an indication that you must put your ideas into action. In the reverse, it indicates delays and setbacks in your venture and less-than-expected progress in whatever you do.

The Page of Wands represents motivation, drive, and enthusiasm. If you draw this card, you'll likely get good news via phone calls or letters shortly. It is a time to think big and take action toward it. In the reverse, the Page of Wands represents bad news and news of setbacks and delays. You could feel unmotivated and uninspired.

The Court Cards of Pentacles

The King of Pentacles stands for generosity and financial stability. If you draw this card, you could feel proud of your achievement and that your hard work and diligence are paying off. You could be reaching the social status you have been dreaming of. In reverse, it could indicate that you are losing control and cannot see the path of your goals clearly.

The Queen of Pentacles stands for thrift and security. If you draw this card, it means prosperity, success, and high financial status. You'll achieve your goals. In the reverse, the Queen of Pentacles stands for poverty and lack of financial stability.

The Knight of Pentacles represents decisiveness and reliability. This card stands for practicality and common sense. It is a card that indicates you'll achieve your dreams through hard work and perseverance. In reverse, it stands for irresponsibility and lack of common sense.

The Page of Pentacles stands for progress and concentration. If you draw this card, you'll likely get good news regarding wealth and money. It is a card that tells you to start the groundwork toward your long-term dreams. In reverse, it could bring bad news regarding money and materialistic matters.

The Court Cards of Swords

The King of Swords signifies maturity and logic. Generally speaking, the King of Swords represents power, authority, and discipline. It deals with ethics and morals, the key elements of a good king. The King of Swords does not like to show any public display of emotion. Drawing this card upright means an environment of structure and order will work well in the current scenario. A reversed King of Swords represents a lack of self-discipline and structure.

The Queen of Swords represents clarity and intelligence. Drawing an upright Queen of Swords could indicate the entry of a wise, old lady offering counsel and protection for you. She is sharp-witted and honest and loves her wards immensely. A reversed Queen of Swords translates to rudeness, malice, and lack of empathy in your life.

The Knight of Swords signifies debate and confrontation. It is also a card of change and tells you that you must jump in and grab the moment. The Knight of Swords is an intellectual, and if this upright card appears in your spread, it means you have a single-minded focus to complete the task at hand. A reversed Knight of Swords means you are missing out on seeing an excellent opportunity because you are out of your depths.

The Page of Swords stands for self-assuredness and invention. The Page of Swords is all about inspiration and planning. If you draw an upright Page of Swords, then it could be an indication to have patience and to think carefully before speaking. In reverse, the Page of Swords indicates a lack of ideas and planning and is defensive and cynical.

With a clear idea of how each card in the tarot decks works and what they signify, it is time to move on and learn how to create spreads and layouts and how to read them accurately.

Chapter 9: Spreads and Layouts

This chapter will teach you the most commonly used tarot spreads (how the cards are laid out for reading).

One-Card Spread

Set the intention and be clear about the answer you seek. Shuffle the deck as you focus on the question. Pull out the card and lay it on the ground, face up. Look at it and see what it is trying to tell you, especially concerning your question. Refer to the meanings of the cards given in the previous chapters of this book for clarity.

Three-Card Spread

When you pull out three cards for this spread, they can have multiple interpretations depending on your search and need. The first, second, and thirds card you draw can indicate the following:

- Past, present, and future
- You, your relationship, your spouse/partner
- The situation, the action that needs to be taken, and the outcome
- You, your current life path, your potential

Again, set the intention clearly, draw out the three cards, place them before you, and interpret their messages and meanings.

The Yes/No Spread

A yes/no spread works differently for different people. Depending on your connection with the cards in your tarot deck, you can choose certain cards to be a yes and certain cards to be a no. For example, if you feel a strong positive connection with the four Aces, you can choose them to signify a Yes to your question. Similarly, you can choose a few cards that could signify a No. Set your intention, ask your question, and pull out cards until you get a Yes or a No card.

The Celtic Cross Spread

The Celtic Cross spread.
ArrowTarot, CC BY-SA 4.0 <https://creativecommons.org/licenses/by-sa/4.0>, via Wikimedia Commons https://commons.wikimedia.org/wiki/File:Celtic_Cross_Tarot_Spread.jpg

The Celtic Cross Spread consists of 10 cards placed in the form of a cross. This spread gives you deep insights into your queries. Set your intent, shuffle the deck well, and start drawing cards and placing them as follows:

- The first card is placed at the center of the cross and deals with the querent or the seeker, their personality, the state of mind, etc.
- The second card is placed across the first card and represents the blocks and obstacles preventing the seeker from getting what they want
- The third card is placed beneath the two center cards and signifies the root or the underlying reason for the blocks and obstacles
- The fourth card is on the left side of the center cards and stands for recent events affecting the question
- The fifth card is put above the center cards and represents the various available possibilities and solutions for the question
- The sixth card is placed to the right of the center cards and gives insights into achieving the desired outcomes
- The above six cards complete the shape of the cross. The next four cards are placed vertically along the right side of the Celtic cross
- The seventh card is the bottommost of the vertical line and gives insights into how the querent sees themselves in a positive or negative light
- The eighth card, placed above the seventh, represents your environment, including family, friends, and others helping you or getting in the way of your goals.
- The ninth card above the eighth stands for your hopes and fears
- The tenth card, which comes right on top of the vertical line, stands for the outcome, which gives you a fairly accurate result when read along with the sixth card

The Tree of Life Spread

The Tree of Life Spread is based on the Kabbalistic Tree of Life form and consists of ten cards corresponding to the ten Sephiroth. Here's a small breakup for your understanding:

Card Numbers 1, 3, and 5 together form a vertical line with 1 at the top and 5 at the bottom. Card Numbers 2, 4, and 6 are aligned respectively with 1, 3, and 5 on their left, and a gap in the middle for card numbers 7, 8, 9, and 10 starting from the bottom. Card 7 is placed slightly below cards 3 and 5, and card number 10 is slightly above cards 1 and 3. The whole form looks like the Kabbalistic Tree of Life. The meanings are as follows:

- **Cards 1 and 2** (aligned horizontally with each other) represent the issue or the query.
- **Cards 3 and 4** represent people or things impacting the issue or query negatively or positively.
- **Cards 5 and 6** represent the querent's feelings and thoughts.
- **Card 7** represents the physical world, including your body, possessions, and other physical and materialistic aspects of your life.
- **Card 8** represents the querent's persona and personality, how the person lives and presents themselves every day.
- **Card 9** represents the advice your heart is giving you.
- **Card 10** signifies the spiritual or moral outcomes and your own growth in these two because of the issue.

The Zodiac Spread

The Zodiac Spread is also known as the 12-House Astrology Spread and requires you to draw out 12 cards and lay them out in a particular way. As usual, set the intention, shuffle the deck, draw out the 12 cards one at a time, and place them as follows:

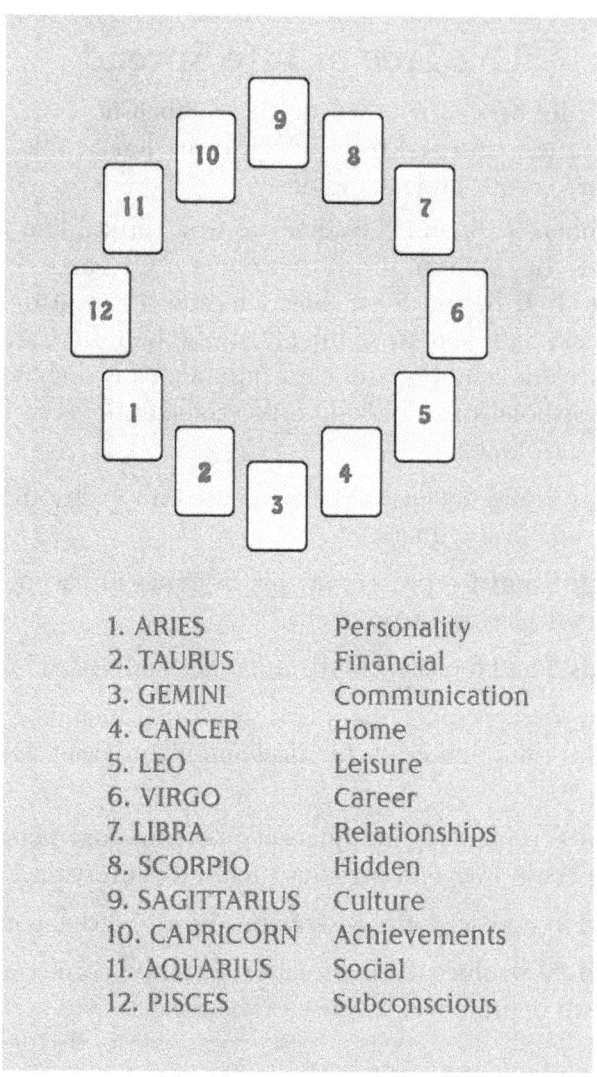

The Zodiac spread.

Place the first card on the far left of the table. This position is called the 9 o'clock point (as it would look in a wall clock). Then place the other counters in a counter-clockwise direction at every hour of the wall clock.

- **The first card** (at the 9 o'clock position) is your sun sign and signifies your life and personality.
- **The second card** (at the 8 o'clock position) represents your wealth and resources. It is the house of self-worth.

- **The third card** (at the 7 o'clock position) determines your environment, including your family, friends, and people at your workplace.
- **The fourth card** (at the 6 o'clock position) is specifically for your home and family.
- **The fifth card** (at the 5 o'clock position) stands for your creativity.
- **The sixth card** (at the 4 o'clock position) represents your daily routine, including self-care, nutrition, exercise, etc.
- **The seventh card** (at the 3 o'clock position) is about your partnerships, including romantic and other relationships. Even enemies are in a relationship with you!
- **The eighth card** (at the 2 o'clock position) signifies your secrets. It involves taboo subjects such as sex, death, and other topics that one doesn't openly discuss.
- **The ninth card** (at the 1 o'clock position) is about your growth and development, including education, long-distance travel, philosophical growth, etc.
- **The tenth card** (at the 12 o'clock position) is about your profession and career. It is also about how you are fulfilling your dreams and aspirations.
- **The eleventh card** (at the 11 o'clock position) covers your community, including people in your community, social circle, acquaintances, etc. It also deals with charity.
- **The twelfth card** (at the 10 o'clock position) deals with your subconscious mind and reflects your hidden fears and burdens.

Conclusion - Reading the Cards

This last concluding chapter gives insights on how to read the cards in a spread through a few examples. Before that, you must learn a grounding ritual and how to set intentions.

Grounding Ritual and Setting Intention

Before you begin a tarot card reading, do this grounding ritual for stability and protection.

1. Sit down, holding the tarot deck in your hand.
2. Close your eyes and visualize roots growing from your seat that hold you firmly to the ground.
3. Imagine these roots supporting you.
4. Then, imagine an orb of white light covering you entirely, keeping you safe from evil and negativity.

Now, open your eyes and set your intention for the card reading. Here are some tips for setting the intention.

- Write down your intentions. What answers do you seek from the card reading?
- Be clear while forming the intentions. What is your desired final outcome?
- The intention can be in the form of dedication, purpose, prayer, or visualization.

- Repeat your intention while shuffling, drawing the cards, and laying them out in your preferred spread choice.

Interpreting the Cards

When the spread is ready, read the cards using the various astrological, Kabbalistic, numerological, and tarot interpretations mentioned in this book. Here are some examples of reading cards from spreads.

If you have a Six of Swords in the 6 o'clock position (the third card) of a Zodiac spread, then it could indicate a move or travel as this card represents your environment, including daily travel and commute.

Getting an Ace card in the 5 o'clock position (the fifth card drawn) could indicate pregnancy if other factors are in order. Aces are for new beginnings; the fifth card deals with home and family.

Look out for combinations in the spread; for example, in a two-card spread, if you get a combination of an Eight of Wands (that signifies travel) and a Six of Cups (that deals with childhood memories and friends), then it could indicate a journey to meet your childhood friends.

If you are looking for a change in employment and get an Ace in your drawing, it could indicate a new job, as an Ace stands for new beginnings.

Watch out for symbols and images depicted in the cards drawn. For example, if you draw a Judgment and Temperance card in the same spread (remember both these cards have images of archangels), it could mean spirit guides or angels are watching over you.

Suppose you draw cards representing the air element and the water element. In that case, it could mean that you need to balance your heart and head for optimal outcomes.

In this way, you can interpret the meanings of the tarot cards by combining all the knowledge from this book. When you finish reading, remember to thank the divine and close your reading.

Some FAQs

Can I do multiple readings, one after another?

Multiple readings, one after another, can give you confusing, conflicting messages. Stick to one reading that you trust.

Should I rest between meetings?

If you have done one tarot reading and are unsure of the meanings, it is recommended that you wait for at least one more month before seeking answers to the same questions.

What if I'm wrong?

Yes, tarot readings can go wrong for various including but not limited to the following:

- As a tarot card reader, your state of mind could be confused and unclear.
- The tarot querent could be imbued with negative energy that is coming in the way of accurate reading.

In such cases, it makes sense to stop the reading, perform grounding rituals one more time, and then read again. If the problem persists, it is best to put off the reading until you feel ready.

Tarot card reading requires continuous practice and relentless connection with your instincts. Keep practicing until you master the wonderful art of tarot reading.

Here's another book by Mari Silva that you might like

Your Free Gift
(only available for a limited time)

Thanks for getting this book! If you want to learn more about various spirituality topics, then join Mari Silva's community and get a free guided meditation MP3 for awakening your third eye. This guided meditation mp3 is designed to open and strengthen ones third eye so you can experience a higher state of consciousness. Simply visit the link below the image to get started.

https://spiritualityspot.com/meditation

References

"12 Astrology Zodiac Signs Dates, Meanings and Compatibility | ZodiacSign.com." Www.zodiacsign.com, www.zodiacsign.com/.

Aliza Kelly Faragher. "12 Zodiac Signs: Personality Traits and Sign Dates." Allure, Allure, 29 Nov. 2018, www.allure.com/story/zodiac-sign-personality-traits-dates.

---. "Am I Psychic? How to Tap into Your Own Psychic Abilities." Allure, Allure, 2 July 2018, www.allure.com/story/am-i-psychic-how-to-tap-into-psychic-abilities.

Alves, Nuno. "The Energy of Spaces and People: How It Works." Energy and Consciousness, 19 Apr. 2015, https://medium.com/energy-and-consciousness/how-energy-works-10893210cc8d

"A Guide to the Planets in Astrology and What They Each Represent." New York Post, 5 Nov. 2021, https://nypost.com/article/astrology-planets-meaning/

Brignac, Wren McMurdo. "What Tarot Cards Represent Which Zodiac Signs? The Story Told by the Major Arcana." Darkdaystarot, 30 Jan. 2022, www.darkdaystarot.com/single-post/what-tarot-cards-represent-which-zodiac-signs-the-story-told-by-the-major-arcana#.

Bunning, Joan. "The Fool's Journey." Www.learntarot.com, www.learntarot.com/journey.htm.

"Chabad.org." @Chabad, 2019, www.chabad.org.

Chanek, Jack. "A Beginner's Guide to Qabalistic Tarot." Llewellyn Worldwide, 9 Dec. 2021, www.llewellyn.com/journal/article/2971.

"Cleansing, Protection & Grounding Methods." Truly Teach Me Tarot, 17 May 2012, https://teachmetarot.com/part-1-minor-arcana/lesson-2/psychic-protection-chakra-cleansing/psychic-protection-supplement/

Coughlin, Sara. "Why You Should Pay Attention to the Court Cards in Your Tarot Deck." Www.refinery29.com, www.refinery29.com/en-us/tarot-court-cards-meaning#slide-4.

CyberAstro.com. "Astrology Benefits in Your Life." Cyberastro, www.cyberastro.com/article/benefits-from-astrology-in-your-life.

David, Lauren. "The 5 Best Tarot Card Decks, according to Professional Tarot Readers." Insider, www.insider.com/guides/hobbies-crafts/best-tarot-cards#the-wild-unknown-tarot-deck-and-guide-set-5.

Deb, Sujata. "Energy Reading Study Guide | How to Read Energy | TheMindFool." TheMindFool - Perfect Medium for Self-Development & Mental Health. Explorer of Lifestyle Choices & Seeker of the Spiritual Journey, 22 Apr. 2020, https://themindfool.com/energy-reading

Ghare, Madhavi. "Structure of a Tarot Card Deck." Tarot-Ically Speaking, 27 Oct. 2010, www.taroticallyspeaking.com/begin/structure-of-a-tarot-card-deck/.

"How to Read a Celtic Cross Tarot Spread." Well+Good, 29 Aug. 2021, www.wellandgood.com/celtic-cross-tarot-spread/.

"Intention-Setting in Tarot Readings (and Everywhere Else)." Practical Magic, www.practicalmagic.co/pm-blog/2021/2/5/intention-setting-in-tarot-readings.

"Introduction to the Tree of Life." Kabbalah Experience, https://kabbalahexperience.com/introduction-to-the-tree-of-life/

"Kabbalah." Glorian, https://glorian.org/learn/topics/kabbalah

Kliegman, Isabel Radow. "Tarot and the Tree of Life." Theosophical Society in America, www.theosophical.org/publications/quest-magazine/1358-tarot-and-the-tree-of-life.

"Learning & Using the Zodiac Tarot Spread." The Simple Tarot, 27 Nov. 2018, https://thesimpletarot.com/learning-using-zodiac-tarot-spread/

Louise, Esther. "Tarot Numerology: Learning the Meanings of Tarot Card Numbers." Through the Phases, 24 Apr. 2020, www.throughthephases.com/tarot-numerology/.

Marina. "Kabbalah and the Tarot - Learn the Connection of Tarot & Kabbalah." City Tarot, 8 Nov. 2018, www.citytarot.com/kabbalah-tarot-minor-arcana/.

---. "The Fool | Tarot Card Meaning." City Tarot, 27 July 2018, www.citytarot.com/tarot-card-meanings-the-fool/.

"Master Number 11 Meaning." Www.numerology.com, www.numerology.com/articles/about-numerology/master-number-11/.

McGarry, Caitlin. "PSA: Your Zodiac Sign Has Its Own Tarot Card." Cosmopolitan, 3 Nov. 2021, www.cosmopolitan.com/lifestyle/a31913908/tarot-cards-zodiac-signs-astrology/.

"Minor Arcana Tarot Card Meanings." Biddy Tarot, www.biddytarot.com/tarot-card-meanings/minor-arcana/.

Parlett, David. "Tarot | Playing Card." Encyclopedia Britannica, 7 Apr. 2009, www.britannica.com/topic/tarot.

"Practical Tree of Life Spread." Mary K. Greer's Tarot Blog, 26 Nov. 2008, https://marykgreer.com/2008/11/25/practical-tree-of-life-spread/

"Tarot.com's Numerology Guide." Tarot.com, www.tarot.com/numerology.

"Tarotscope: How Astrology and the Tarot Are Linked." Two Wander, www.twowander.com/blog/tarotscope-how-astrology-and-tarot-are-linked.

"The Fool Meaning - Major Arcana Tarot Card Meanings." Labyrinthos, https://labyrinthos.co/blogs/tarot-card-meanings-list/the-fool-meaning-major-arcana-tarot-card-meanings

"The Minor Arcana." Thetarotguide, www.thetarotguide.com/minor-arcana.

"The Pros and Cons of Tarot Cards for Mental Health." Healthline, 4 June 2021, www.healthline.com/health/mind-body/tarot-card-can-help-your-mental-health-or-hurt-it#takeaway.

"The Tarot and the Tree of Life Correspondences." Labyrinthos, https://labyrinthos.co/blogs/learn-tarot-with-labyrinthos-academy/the-tarot-and-the-tree-of-life-correspondences

"Thoth Tarot 101: Let This Amazing Deck Guide Your Life." Www.alittlesparkofjoy.com, 16 Sept. 2021, www.alittlesparkofjoy.com/thoth-tarot/.

Wheel of Fortune Tarot Card Meanings. 31 Jan. 2020, https://tarotoak.com/wheel-of-fortune-tarot-card-meaning/

Wigington, Patti. "Where Did Tarot Cards Come From?" Learn Religions, 2018, www.learnreligions.com/a-brief-history-of-tarot-2562770.

Metmuseum.org, 2019, www.metmuseum.org/blogs/in-season/2016/tarot

www.ingramcontent.com/pod-product-compliance
Lightning Source LLC
Chambersburg PA
CBHW051846160426
43209CB00006B/1181